SCHOLASTIC

National Curriculum
MATHS
Revision Guide

✔ Recap
✔ Revise
✔ Skills Check

Ages 9–10
Year 5

KS2

SCHOLASTIC

National Curriculum
MATHS
Revision Guide

Book End, Range Road, Witney, Oxfordshire, OX29 0YD
Registered office: Westfield Road, Southam, Warwickshire CV47 0RA
www.scholastic.co.uk

5 6 7 8 9   8 9 0 1 2 3 4 5

British Library Cataloguing-in-Publication Data
A catalogue record for this book is available from the British Library.

ISBN 978-1407-15989-8
Printed in Malaysia

Author
Paul Hollin

Editorial
Rachel Morgan, Jenny Wilcox, Mark Walker, Red Door Media Ltd,
Kate Baxter, Margaret Eaton and Julia Roberts

Series Design
Scholastic Design Team: Nicolle Thomas and Neil Salt

Design
Oxford Designers & Illustrators

Cover Design
Scholastic Design Team: Nicolle Thomas and Neil Salt

Cover Illustration
Shutterstock / © VIGE.CO

Illustration
Simon Walmesley

Contents

Measurement

Geometry

Statistics

How to use this book

Introduction

This book has been written to help children reinforce the mathematics they have learned at school. It provides information and varied examples, activities and questions in a clear and consistent format across 39 units, covering all of National Curriculum for Mathematics for this age group.

I give tips to children and adults alike!

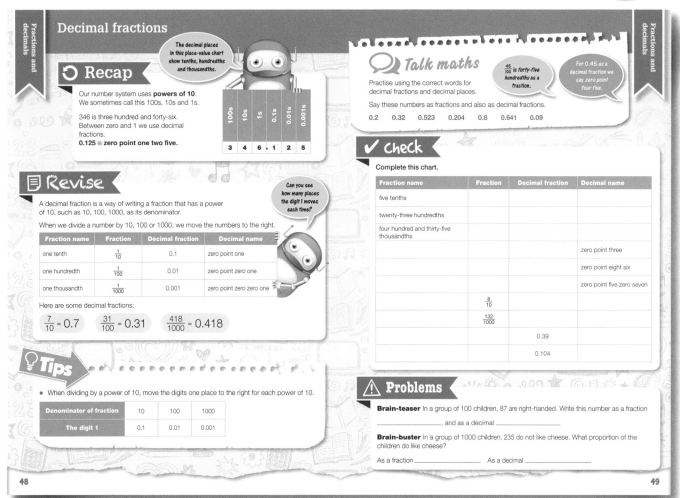

Unit structure

- **Recap** – a recap of basic facts of the mathematical area in focus.
- **Revise** – examples and facts specific to the age group.
- **Tips** – short and simple advice to aid understanding.
- **Talk maths** – focused activities that encourage verbal practice.
- **Check** – a focused range of questions, with answers at the end of the book.
- **Problems** – word problems requiring mathematics to be used in context.

* Note that Tips and Talk maths sections are not present in single-page units.

Keep some blank or squared paper handy for notes and calculations!

Using this book at home

Improving your child's maths

It sounds obvious, but this is the best reason for using this book. Whether working sequentially through units, dipping in to resolve confusion, or reinforcing classroom learning, you can use this book to help your child see the benefits and pleasures of being competent in maths.

Consolidating school work

Most schools communicate clearly what they are doing each week via newsletters or homework. Using this book, alongside the maths being done at school, can boost children's mastery of the concepts.

Be sure not to get ahead of schoolwork or to confuse your child. If in doubt, talk to your child's class teacher.

Revising for tests

Regular testing is a fact of life for children these days, like it or not. Improving children's confidence is a good way to avoid stress as well as improve performance. Where children have obvious difficulties, dipping in to the book and focusing on specific facts and skills can be very helpful. To provide specific practice for end-of-year tests we recommend *National Curriculum Maths Tests for Year 5*.

Do a little, often

Keep sessions to an absolute maximum of 30 minutes. Even if children want to keep going, short amounts of focused study on a regular basis will help to sustain learning and enthusiasm in the long run.

Track progress

The revision tracker chart on page 7 provides a simple way for children to record their progress with this book. Remember, you've really 'got it' when you can understand and apply the maths confidently in different contexts. This means all the questions in the *Check* and *Problems* sections should not present any difficulties.

Avoid confusion

If your child really doesn't seem to understand a particular unit, take a step back. There may be some prior knowledge that s/he does not understand, or it may contradict how they have learned similar facts at school. Try looking at much simpler examples than those given in the book, and if in doubt talk to your child's teacher.

Talk, talk, talk

There is big value in discussing maths, both using vocabulary and explaining concepts. The more children can be encouraged to do this, especially explaining their thinking and understanding, the better the learning. Even if adults understand the work better than children, having them 'teach' you is a great way to consolidate their learning.

Practice makes perfect

Even the world's best footballers have to regularly practise kicking a ball. Brief warm-ups before starting a unit, such as rapid recall of times tables or addition facts, or answering a few questions on mathematical vocabulary (see glossary) can help keep children on their toes.

Maths is everywhere – use it!

Children have lots of English lessons at school, and they use language almost constantly in daily life. They also have lots of maths lessons but encounter its use in daily life much less. Involving children in everyday maths is very useful. Shopping and money are the obvious ones, but cooking, decorating, planning holidays, catching buses, to name a few examples, can all involve important mathematical thinking and talk.

Revision tracker

	Not sure	Getting there	Got it!
Identify and use number facts to at least 1,000,000			
Count in powers of 10 up to 1,000,000			
Count using positive and negative whole numbers			
Round any number up to the nearest power of 10			
Read Roman numerals to 1000 (M)			
Use mental methods to add and subtract			
Add large numbers using formal written methods			
Subtract large numbers using formal written methods			
Identify multiples, factor pairs and common factors			
Work with prime numbers			
Use formal methods for long multiplication			
Use formal methods for long division			
Use mental methods to multiply and divide numbers			
Recognise and use square and cube numbers			
Multiply and divide numbers by 10, 100 and 1000			
Use multiplication and division to scale up and down and to find the rate at which something happens			
Solve multi-step calculations and problems			
Compare and order fractions			
Recognise and use mixed numbers and improper fractions			
Add and subtract fractions			
Multiply proper fractions and mixed numbers by whole numbers			
Convert simple fractions into decimals and vice versa			
Use thousandths, hundredths, and tenths as fractions or decimals			
Understand numbers with up to three decimal places			
Round decimals to the nearest whole number or one decimal place			
Understand and use simple percentages			
Convert between different units of length			
Measure and calculate the perimeters of shapes			
Calculate and estimate the areas of shapes			
Convert between different units of mass, capacity and volume			
Convert between different units of time			
Solve money problems			
Identify 3D shapes			
Work with acute, obtuse and reflex angles			
Identify angles in steps of 90°			
Identify different shapes using facts about their sides and angles			
Reflect and translate shapes			
Make and use line graphs			
Read, complete and interpret information in tables			

Numbers up to 1,000,000

What do the other digits represent?

↺ Recap

23,471 in words is twenty-three thousand, four hundred and seventy-one.

10,000s	1000s	100s	10s	1s
2	3	4	7	1

The **place value** of the **3** digit represents **3000**, the **4** represents **400**.

📄 Revise

What number does each of the digits represent?

1,000,000s	100,000s	10,000s	1000s	100s	10s	1s
	3	4	0	2	6	1

This number is three hundred and forty thousand, two hundred and sixty-one.
Now read these statements aloud. They are both true.

For this symbol: > say *is bigger than* and for this symbol: < say *is smaller than*.

999,999 > 703,374 > 12,029 > 7698   6418 < 30,206 < 163,192 < 1,000,000

💡 Tips

Hey there! Follow my tips and you'll soon find big numbers are not a big problem!

- Write the place-value headings in columns above numbers if you're stuck.
- Use commas in numbers over a hundred thousand (100,000) and numbers over ten thousand (10,000).
- If you get mixed up with the > and < symbols, just think of the symbol as the mouth of a crocodile – the crocodile always eats the bigger number!

876,457 292,345

Talk maths

100,000   1,000,000

Read these numbers and statements aloud.

1000   10,000   324,492 > 27,920

500,000   999,999

725 < 4205

DID YOU KNOW?

Did you know that 500,000 is half a million?

✔ Check

1. Write this number in words: 34,805.

_____

2. Write this number in digits.
   Two hundred and thirty-seven thousand, one hundred and twenty _____

3. What does the 4 digit represent in 540,371? _____

4. Put these numbers in order, from smallest to largest.
   25,612   50,000   725   7   225,421   1,000,000   12   899,372

_____

5. Insert the correct sign, < or >, between these pairs of numbers.

   a. 3521 _____ 5630   **b.** 15,204 _____ 9798   **c.** 833,521 _____ 795,732

⚠ Problems

Football club	Fintan United	Forest Rovers	Winchcomb City
Fans	500,243	96,589	742,104

Brain-teaser Which club has the most fans? _____

Brain-buster Write the clubs in order, from largest to smallest, according to the number of fans.

_____   _____   _____

Counting in steps up to 1,000,000

↻ Recap

When we count in steps, we add or subtract the same number each time.

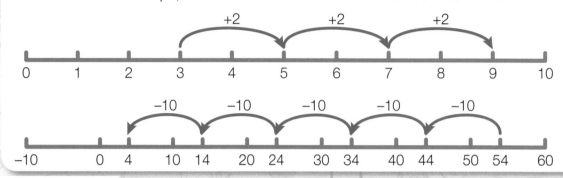

📄 Revise

Powers of 10 are numbers that are made by multiplying 10 by 10 a number of times:

- 100 is 10 × 10 or 10 to the power of 2 (10²)
- 1000 is 10 × 10 × 10 or 10 to the power of 3 (10³)
- 10,000 is 10 × 10 × 10 × 10 or 10 to the power of 4 (10⁴)

We can count on or back in steps for any power of 10.

Can you continue the count?

This number line goes up to 1000. Starting at 45, we count in steps of 100.

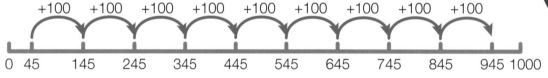

| +100 | +100 | +100 | +100 | +100 | +100 | +100 | +100 | +100 |

0 45   145   245   345   445   545   645   745   845   945 1000

This number line goes up to 60,000. Starting at 1362, we count in steps of 10,000.

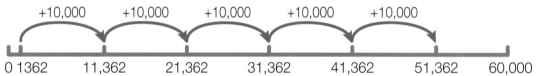

| +10,000 | +10,000 | +10,000 | +10,000 | +10,000 |

0 1362   11,362   21,362   31,362   41,362   51,362   60,000

Can you count back in ten thousands? Try starting at 51,362.

💡 Tips

- Write the place values in columns above numbers if you're stuck.
- Remember which power of 10 you are adding each time.

0   200,000   400,000   600,000   800,000   1,000,000
    100,000   300,000   500,000   700,000   900,000

- Choose a number less than 1000, then try counting on in 100,000s.

Count aloud in steps of different powers of 10.

Talk maths

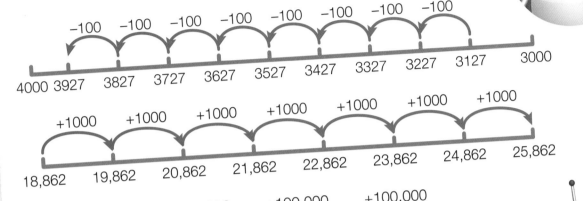

+100,000, +100,000, +100,000, +100,000

521,604   621,604   721,604   821,604   921,604   1,000,000

Can you continue counting and say what the next three numbers would be?

✔ Check

1. Complete this sequence, counting on in steps of 100.

   124, _____, _____, _____, _____, _____

2. Complete this sequence, counting back in steps of 1000.

   12,906, _____, _____, _____, _____, _____

3. Complete this sequence, counting on in steps of 100,000.

   320,435, _____, _____, _____, _____, _____

4. Complete this sequence, counting back in steps of 10,000.

   243,000, _____, _____, _____, _____, _____

⚠ Problems

Brain-teaser Evie's mum is saving for a family holiday. She has already saved £746 and will continue to save £100 a month. How many more months of saving will it take before she has over £2000?

_____

Brain-buster There are 123,456 people at a football match. At the end of the match 10,000 people leave every ten minutes. How many people will still be in the stadium 50 minutes after the match has finished?

_____

Positive and negative numbers

On a number line, when we add numbers we move to the right; when we take away numbers we move to the left.

↺ Recap

Numbers less than zero are called negative numbers.
Numbers more than zero are called positive numbers.

−5   −4   −3   −2   −1   0   1   2   3   4   5

📄 Revise

Temperature is a great way to practise using positive and negative numbers.

- If you start at +5 and count back 5 you stop at 0.
- If you start at −8 and count on 6 you stop at −2.
- If you start at −3 and count on 4 you stop at +1.
- If you start at +2 and count back 10 you stop at −8.

We can do simple calculations with positive and negative numbers.
For example, **2 − 3 = −1**   Or, **−3 + 2 = −1**

Try a few of your own and check them with a friend.

+10
+9
+8
+7
+6
+5
+4
+3
+2
+1
0
−1
−2
−3
−4
−5
−6
−7
−8
−9
−10

💡 Tips

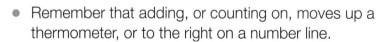

I'm positive my tips will help you!

- Remember that adding, or counting on, moves up a thermometer, or to the right on a number line.

−10 −9 −8 −7 −6 −5 −4 −3 −2 −1 0 1 2 3 4 5 6 7 8 9 10

- Use your finger to count on and back from different numbers. Each time say your calculation aloud, such as **minus four add seven equals plus three**.

💬 Talk maths

Make sure you understand the different vocabulary for talking about positive and negative numbers. Read these statements aloud.

> We say count on, plus or add.

> We say count back, minus or subtract.

> We say minus three to subtract three, but we also say minus three to talk about the number −3. We also say negative 3 to talk about the number −3.

> We can say positive or plus for numbers greater than zero, but usually we just say the number.

> We always say negative or minus for numbers less than zero.

> We say plus five to add five, but we also say plus five to talk about the number 5.

✔ Check

```
−10 −9 −8 −7 −6 −5 −4 −3 −2 −1  0  1  2  3  4  5  6  7  8  9  10
```

1. Complete these calculations.

    a. −5 + 5 = _____   **b.** 5 − 5 = _____   **c.** −2 − 7 = _____   **d.** 3 − 7 = _____

2. Count on from −6 to +6 in steps of 2. Write down each number.

    _____ , _____ , _____ , _____ , _____ , _____ , _____

3. Insert the missing signs, + or −.

    a. 4 _____ 4 = 0   **b.** −5 _____ 6 = 1   **c.** 2 _____ 7 = 9   **d.** 2 _____ 8 = −6

4. Insert the missing numbers.

    a. −3 + _____ = 1   **b.** 1 − _____ = −2   **c.** _____ − 7 = 2   **d.** _____ − 10 = −8

⚠ Problems

Brain-teaser The temperature at dusk is 4 degrees Celsius (4°C). If the temperature drops 6°C by midnight, what will the temperature be? _____

Brain-buster In January, the temperature at 11am in Montreal, Canada, was −9°C and in Sydney, Australia, it was 27°C. What was the difference in temperature?

_____

Rounding numbers

Don't forget, 34 and below round down to 30, 35 and above round up to 40.

↻ Recap

To round a number to the nearest 10 we can look at its position on the number line.

Don't forget (again!), 50 and 500 round up, 49 and 499 round down.

30   32   37   40

We then look for the nearest 10.

32 rounds down to 30   **37 rounds up to 40**

We can do the same with 100s and 1000s.

355 rounds up to 400   **1268 rounds down to 1000**

355
300   400

1268
1000   2000

🗐 Revise

It isn't hard, you just need to think about where they are on the number line.

We often round numbers to the nearest power of 10 (that's 10, 100, 1000, 10,000, 100,000, and so on).

Rounding to the nearest 10,000: 4235 rounds down to zero and 6249 rounds up to 10,000.

4235   6249
0   10,000

Rounding to the nearest 100,000: 344,235 rounds down to 300,000 and 689,249 rounds up to 700,000.

344,235   689,249
0   500,000   1,000,000

💡Tips

- Always think carefully about what you want to round to: nearest 10, 100, 1000 and so on, and then think about the part of the number line the number is on. So:
  635,850 rounds to the nearest 10 as 635,850
  635,850 rounds to the nearest 100 as 635,900
  635,850 rounds to the nearest 1000 as 636,000
  635,850 rounds to the nearest 10,000 as 640,000
  635,850 rounds to the nearest 100,000 as 600,000

Talk maths

347,248 rounded to the nearest 1000 is 347,000.

Write six different numbers between zero and one million. Read aloud each number to a friend and challenge them to round it to each power of 10 from 10 to 10,000.

What is 54,250 rounded to the nearest 100?

✔ Check

Complete the table below.

	Rounded to nearest 10	Rounded to nearest 100	Rounded to nearest 1000	Rounded to nearest 10,000	Rounded to nearest 100,000
67					
145					
3320					
78,249					
381,082					
555,555					

⚠ Problems

Brain-teaser 54,527 people watch a football match.
What is this rounded to the nearest 10,000? _____

Brain-buster A famous footballer normally gets paid £346,000 per match! If he scores a goal his pay is rounded up to the next 100,000. If he doesn't score a goal it is rounded down to the nearest 100,000. How much does he lose if he doesn't score, and how much does he gain if he does?

Loss if fails to score: £_____ ; Gain if scores: £_____

Roman numerals

What are the rules for making 4 and 9 with Roman numerals?

↻ Recap

Look at the clock and check that you know the Roman numerals for numbers 1–12.

▤ Revise

Number	1	2	3	4	5	6	7	8	9	10
Roman numeral	I	II	III	IV	V	VI	VII	VIII	IX	X
Number	11	12	13	14	15	16	17	18	19	20
Roman numeral	XI	XII	XIII	XIV	XV	XVI	XVII	XVIII	IXX	XX
Number	30	40	50	60	70	80	90	100	500	1000
Roman numeral	XXX	XL	L	LX	LXX	LXXX	XC	C	D	M

✔ Check

With a bit of brain power, you can use this chart to find out any Roman numeral up to 1000!

1. Write these Roman numerals in numbers.

   a. VIII _____   **b.** XXIII _____   **c.** CCC _____   **d.** XCV _____

   e. CIV _____   **f.** CXL _____   **g.** DCX _____   **h.** CM _____

2. Write these numbers in their Roman numeral equivalent.

   a. 22 _____   **b.** 1 _____   **c.** 55 _____   **d.** 93 _____

   e. 112 _____   **f.** 160 _____   **g.** 212 _____   **h.** 965 _____

⚠ Problems

Brain-buster The Romans left Britain in the year AD410, 465 years after they first arrived. Use Roman numerals to write the date they left, and the number of years they spent in Britain.

Date: _____   Years in Britain: _____

Mental methods for adding and subtracting

↻ Recap

You will probably know several ways of doing mental calculations.

You must know your number bonds: $7 + 8 = 15$ $15 - 8 = 7$ $15 - 7 = 8$

Partitioning numbers is important too: **$25 + 12 = 37$**

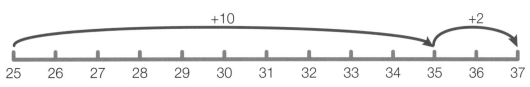

```
        +10                              +2
 ┌──────────────────────────────┐   ┌──────┐
 25  26  27  28  29  30  31  32  33  34  35  36  37
```

📄 Revise

Remember, adding 99 is easy: add 100 and take away 1!

Mental methods can work just as well for larger numbers, but you need to be confident and know your limits!

$45{,}356 + 12{,}103$ ✓	There is no carrying necessary; just add each column.
$123{,}729 + 943{,}509$ ✗	Too much carrying!
$34{,}302 - 8753$ ✗	Too much carrying!
$16{,}583 - 8000$ ✓	The 100s, 10s and 1s stay exactly the same!

✔ Check

1. Add these numbers using mental methods.

    a. $46 + 50 =$ _____
    b. $127 + 99 =$ _____

    c. $3274 + 2002 =$ _____
    d. $2500 + 7454 =$ _____

    e. $120{,}000 + 10{,}320 =$ _____

2. Subtract these numbers using mental methods.

    a. $80 - 46 =$ _____
    b. $160 - 65 =$ _____

    c. $345 - 99 =$ _____
    d. $4000 - 2500 =$ _____

    e. $275{,}675 - 10{,}000 =$ _____

⚠ Problems

Brain-teaser Jason has read 123 pages of his book. If he reads another 150 pages he will finish it. How many pages does the book have altogether?

_____

Brain-buster Armchairs cost £299 and sofas cost £499. How much would two armchairs and one sofa cost altogether?

_____

Adding large numbers

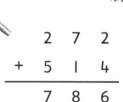

We can arrange numbers in their place-value columns.

↺ Recap

There are formal written methods for adding numbers. You may have been taught methods a bit different to this one. You should use whichever method you are comfortable with – as long as you get the right answer!

```
    2 7 2
  + 5 1 4
  -------
    7 8 6
```

📄 Revise

We know that the place-value columns continue for 1000s, 10,000s, 100,000s and so on.

We can use formal written methods using these columns.

1,000,000s	10,000s	1000s	100s	10s	1s
6	6	4	5	7	2
+ 1	5	3	0	5	4
8	1	7	6	2	6

Don't forget, you can add as many numbers as you like in the columns!

💡 Tips

If in doubt, work it out!

- Lay out your work neatly, showing the + sign and carefully exchanging the numbers between columns.

- When adding two or more numbers some people prefer to write the larger number in the top row of the calculation, but it really doesn't matter which way round you arrange them – the answer will always be the same!

```
    4 1 8 2 1 6
  + 3 2 5 2 7 4
  -------------
    7 4 3 4 9 0
```

💬 Talk maths

Look at the addition below and talk it through aloud, explaining how each stage was done. Make sure you work in the correct order.

```
    2  3  7  1  6  2
+   4  8  4  7  5  3
─────────────────────
    7  2  1  9  1  5
       ı  ı     ı
```

Use estimation to quickly see if your answers are about right.

2435 + 809 is around 2500 + 1000, so the answer will be around 3500.

In fact, 2435 + 809 = 3244 so my estimate was close!

✔ Check

1. Complete each of these additions.

a.
	2	4	3	5
+		8	0	9

b.
	7	4	3	2
+	4	8	7	7

c.
	2	4	3	5	7
+	4	5	8	2	3

d.
	2	4	5	0	2	0
+	3	7	6	2	0	9

2. Use squared paper to write and complete each of these additions.

a. 2459 + 3507

b. 23,417 + 46,219

c. 124,467 + 89,458

d. 231,472 + 238,419 + 121,615 + 67,424

⚠ Problems

Brain-teaser This chart shows the populations of three imaginary cities.

City	Bim	Bam	Bom
Population	236,325	143,544	367,269

Are the combined populations of Bim and Bam larger than the population of Bom? _____

Brain-buster If the population of each city increased by 50,000 people, would the total population of the three cities be more than one million people? _____

Subtracting large numbers

↺ Recap

There are formal written methods for subtracting numbers. You may have been taught methods a bit different to this one. You should use whichever method you are comfortable with – as long as you get the right answers!

```
   ³4̶ ¹1  5
 −  2  3  4
 ─────────
    1  8  1
```

Notice how we exchange one 100 for ten 10s.

📄 Revise

Just like with addition, we can use the place-value columns to help us subtract larger numbers.

1,000,000s	10,000s	1000s	100s	10s	1s
²3̶	¹³4̶	¹⁰1̶	¹2	4	6
− 1	6	5	3	0	4
1	7	5	9	4	2

You need to be very careful at each stage of a written subtraction. Look at this one:

```
   ⁵6̶ ¹²3̶ ⁹0̶ ¹2 ³4̶ ¹5
 −   2   3   5   4  2  9
 ────────────────────────
     3   9   4   8  1  6
```

Look at what you must do if you want to exchange ten of one number for a larger number but the next column has a zero.

💡 Tips

Here are some useful subtraction hints.

- Remember, you can check your subtractions by adding your answer to the number you took away.
  243 − 175 = 68   checking…   **68 + 175 = 243**   correct!

- If you have a method you like, stick to it, practise it, and always check your answers.

Talk maths

Look at the subtraction below and talk it through aloud, explaining how each stage was done. Make sure you work in the correct order.

$$
\begin{array}{r}
{}^3\cancel{4}\ {}^1 3\ 5\ 5\ {}^5\cancel{6}\ {}^1 2 \\
-\ 2\ 4\ 5\ 4\ 2\ 6 \\
\hline
1\ 9\ 0\ 1\ 3\ 6 \\
\hline
\end{array}
$$

Use estimation to quickly see if your answers are *about right*.

1405 – 950 is around 1400 – 900, so the answer will be around 500.

In fact, 1405 – 950 = 455, so my estimate was close!

✔ Check

1. Complete each of these subtractions.

   a.
	3	7	4
−	2	3	5

   b.
	7	4	2	8
−	3	2	6	5

   c.
	4	3	2	6	2	5
−	2	4	3	2	0	6

2. Use squared paper to write out and complete each of these subtractions.

   a. 235 − 116

   b. 4823 − 2550

   c. 13,274 − 9306

   d. 10,206 − 6345

   e. 240,231 − 123,308

⚠ Problems

Brain-teaser This chart shows the populations of three imaginary cities.

City	Bim	Bam	Bom
Population	236,325	143,544	367,269

Which is bigger, the difference between the populations of Bim and Bam, or the difference between the populations of Bim and Bom? _____

Brain-buster There is a fourth city called Bem. It has a population that is 154,289 less than Bom. What is the population of Bem? _____

Multiples and factors

> Factors are the numbers that we multiply together to get multiples.

↻ Recap

A **multiple** is a number that is made by multiplying two numbers.

$4 \times 3 = 12$

12 is a **multiple** of 3, and it is also a **multiple** of 4.
We can also say that 3 and 4 are **factors** of 12.

Revise

Factors are easiest to find as pairs.

$12 = (1 \times 12), (2 \times 6)$ or (3×4)

So the factors of 12 are 1, 2, 3, 4, 6 and 12.

$15 = (1 \times 15)$ or (3×5)

So the factors of 15 are 1, 3, 5 and 15.

Sometimes two different numbers will share the same factor.
We call this a **common factor**.

3 is a common factor of 12 and 15.

> Remember, we can also say that 12 is a multiple of 1, 2, 3, 4 and 6.

> We can also say that 12 and 15 are common multiples of 3.

💡 Tips

> Here's some help with multiples and factors.

- Remember, factors divide into multiples.
  3 is a factor of 12, and 12 is a multiple of 3.
- Some numbers have lots of factors; some only have 2.
- All prime numbers only have themselves and 1 as factors.
- A factor that is *also* a prime number is called, wait for it, a *prime factor*!

💬 Talk maths

Close this book, and then explain to an adult what a factor is and what a multiple is. Use examples to help you.

Then open the book and check how you did.

DID YOU KNOW?

Did you know that multiples go on forever? Don't try it out, just trust me!

✔ Check

1. Write down all the factors of 6. _____

2. Write down five multiples of 4. _____

3. Write all the factor pairs for each of these numbers.

   a. 15 _____   b. 27 _____

   c. 24 _____   d. 30 _____

4. Find the common factors of these numbers.

   a. 12 and 16 _____   b. 15 and 20 _____

   c. 28 and 40 _____   d. 50 and 100 _____

⚠ Problems

Brain-teaser Selina has 24 small chocolates and she wants to share them equally with some of her friends. Complete the chart to show how many children she **could** share them equally between, and how many chocolates each person would get.

Children	1	2						
Chocolates	24	12						

What would happen if Selina tried to share her chocolates between five friends?

_____

Brain-buster Everyone knows there are 365 days in a year, and 7 days in a week.

Are there exactly 52 weeks in a year? _____

Explain your answer. _____

Prime numbers

1 is not counted as a prime number.

Recap

A number that can only be divided by itself or 1, with no remainder, is called a prime number. For example, 2, 3 and 5 are all prime numbers.

2 is the only even prime number. All other even numbers can be divided by 2 as well as 1 and themselves.

Revise

~~1~~	②	③	~~4~~	⑤	~~6~~	⑦	~~8~~	~~9~~	~~10~~
⑪	~~12~~	⑬	~~14~~	~~15~~	~~16~~	⑰	~~18~~	⑲	~~20~~
~~21~~	~~22~~	㉓	~~24~~	~~25~~	~~26~~	~~27~~	~~28~~	㉙	~~30~~
㉛	~~32~~	~~33~~	~~34~~	~~35~~	~~36~~	㊲	~~38~~	~~39~~	~~40~~
㊶	~~42~~	㊸	~~44~~	~~45~~	~~46~~	㊼	~~48~~	~~49~~	~~50~~
~~51~~	~~52~~	(53)	~~54~~	~~55~~	~~56~~	~~57~~	~~58~~	(59)	~~60~~
(61)	~~62~~	~~63~~	~~64~~	~~65~~	~~66~~	(67)	~~68~~	~~69~~	~~70~~
(71)	~~72~~	(73)	~~74~~	~~75~~	~~76~~	~~77~~	~~78~~	(79)	~~80~~
~~81~~	~~82~~	(83)	~~84~~	~~85~~	~~86~~	~~87~~	~~88~~	(89)	~~90~~
~~91~~	~~92~~	~~93~~	~~94~~	~~95~~	~~96~~	(97)	~~98~~	~~99~~	~~100~~

Look at the numbers 1 to 10. We can circle 2 as a prime number. We know that all even numbers can be divided by 2, so we can delete all other even numbers because we know that none of these can be prime numbers.

We can also circle 3, and then delete 9. We know from the times tables that 9 can be divided by 3, so it cannot be a prime number.

I have circled all the prime numbers for you.

Tips

- There are rules that can help you decide if any number is a prime or not.
- A number that is even can be divided by 2, so no even numbers are prime numbers, except 2 itself of course!
- Add the digits of the number together. If the sum can be divided by 3, so can the number, and so it is not a prime number, for example 207: 2 + 0 + 7 = 9, 9 can be divided by 3, so 207 is not a prime number!
- If a number ends in 0 or 5 it can be divided by 5, so it is not a prime number, for example 115 is not a prime number.

Warning!
These rules only *help* you to decide, you may still need to check for other prime factors!

Talk maths

97

Challenge an adult or a friend to a game of *Prime Time*. You need something to time minutes on, such as a stopwatch. You will also need a pencil and paper, for keeping scores and remembering which numbers have been used.

Take it in turns to say a number and challenge the other player to decide whether it is a prime number or not, and record how long it took to answer the question. If challenged, a player must prove why their answer is yes or no, with a sensible explanation.

5
2
11
41

Play Prime Time!

DID YOU KNOW?

Mathematicians are still discovering new prime numbers. Imagine how enormous those numbers must be!

✔ Check

1. What is a prime number? _____

2. Write all the prime numbers between 1 and 20 (there are eight altogether).

   _____

3. Say which of these numbers are prime, and explain each of your answers.

   a. 25 _____

   b. 71 _____

   c. 87 _____

4. Can you think of a prime number greater than 100? _____

⚠ Problems

Brain-teaser 77 cannot be divided by 2, 3 or 5. Does this make it a prime number? Explain your answer.

_____

Brain-buster Mohammed says that 7 is a prime number, and so is 17, so 27 must also be a prime number. Explain why he is wrong.

_____

Multiplying large numbers

Remember, the numbers are arranged in their place-value columns.

↻ Recap

There are formal written methods for multiplying numbers. You may have been taught methods a bit different to this one. You should use whichever method you are comfortable with – as long as you get the right answers!

	6	3
×		7
4	4	1
	2	

	3	2	5
×			6
1	9	5	0
		1	3

	4	6	2	5
×				5
2	3	1	2	5
		3	1	2

📄 Revise

We know that the place-value columns continue for thousands, ten-thousands, hundred-thousands and so on. We can use formal written methods using these columns.

When multiplying two numbers larger than 10, multiply each digit on the top by each digit on the bottom, carrying numbers to the next column along, when necessary.

You can multiply first by the 10s, or the 1s; the answer will still be the same.

We call this long multiplication.

		4	6
	×	1	5
	2	3³	0
	4	6	0	+
	6	9	0

Answer: 690

💡 Tips

- Most people find it easier to put the larger number on the top, although it doesn't really matter which way round you arrange them – the answer will still be the same.
- Remember, the 1 digit in 14 is 10.
- It doesn't matter if you start with the 10s or the 1s.

		3	2	
	×	1	4	
(32 × 4)	1	2	8	
(32 × 10)	3	2	0	+
	4	4	8	

OR

		3	2	
	×	1	4	
(32 × 10)	3	2	0	
(32 × 4)	1	2	8	+
	4	4	8	

Talk maths

> **Remember** that zeros still have to be multiplied, and anything times zero is zero!

Look at the long multiplications below and talk them through aloud, saying how each stage was done.

	3	2	5			2	7				4	3				4	3	6
×			3		×	2	1			×	3	5			×		2	1
	9	7	5			2	7			2	1ˡ	5			4	3	6
		ˡ			5ˡ	4	0	+	1	2	9	0	+	8	7ˡ	2	0	+
					5	6	7		1	5	0	5		9	1	5	6
										ˡ				ˡ		

 **Check**

1. Complete each of these long multiplications.

   a.

	2	1
×	1	3

   b.

	2	3
×	2	4

   c.

	4	5
×	3	1

   d.

	6	3
×	5	6

2. On squared paper, write out and complete each of these long multiplications.

   a. 15 × 21   **b.** 26 × 32   **c.** 53 × 15   **d.** 33 × 40

⚠ Problems

Brain-teaser A school's tuck shop sells cartons of fruit juice. Each carton cost 15p.

If 43 cartons are sold, how much money will be collected? _____

Brain-buster There are 475 children in a school. The school is raising money for charity with a sponsored walk, and they hope to raise £6000. If each child raises £13 will they hit their target? Explain your answer.

_____

_____

Dividing large numbers

↺ Recap

There are formal written methods for dividing numbers. You may have been taught methods a bit different to this one. You should use whichever method you are comfortable with – as long as you get the right answers!

		1	2					2	4	
	3	3	6				4	9	¹6	

For 36 ÷ 3 = 12 we say 36 divided *by* 3 equals 12.

📄 Revise

In short division we move forward remainders. Sometimes there is a remainder at the end.

		1	2	r1				2	4	r3
	3	3	7				4	9	¹9	

We can still use short division when we are dividing by 2-digit numbers. We just need to look for the first whole number that the 2-digit number can divide into, the rest is the same.

		0	2	1	r3			0	3	2	r11
1	2	2	²5	¹5			1	5	4	⁴9	⁴1

💡 Tips

- Lay out your work carefully. Use squared paper to help you.

- You can always check your answer by multiplying the answer by the number you divided by, and then add the remainder.

Talk maths

Remember that zero divided by anything is zero.

Look at this division and talk it through aloud, saying how each stage was done.

		1	2	4	r3
4	4	9	¹9	

✔ Check

1. Complete each of these divisions.

a.
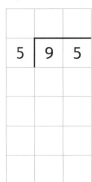

5	9	5

b.

6	6	8

c.
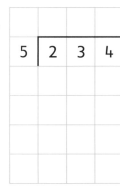

5	2	3	4

d.
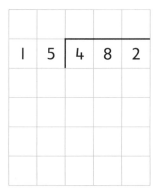

1	5	4	8	2

2. On squared paper, write out and complete each of these divisions.

a. 98 ÷ 7　　　b. 125 ÷ 5　　　c. 522 ÷ 8　　　d. 318 ÷ 15

⚠ Problems

Brain-teaser There are 500 staples in a box. If the teacher's staple gun holds 40 staples, how many times can she refill her staple gun? _____

Brain-buster Mako makes a large bowl of popcorn for her class party. If there are 246 pieces of popcorn, and there are 21 children in the class, how many pieces of popcorn will each child get if it is divided equally?

_____

Mako's teacher eats any remaining pieces. How many pieces does he get? _____

Mental methods for multiplying and dividing

↻ Recap

You know how to use a multiplication square.

Multiplication squares help to show us that division is the *inverse* of multiplication.

So, we can say

$6 \times 7 = 42$ $7 \times 6 = 42$

$42 \div 6 = 7$ $42 \div 7 = 6$

×	1	2	3	4	5	6	7	8	9	10
1	1	2	3	4	5	6	7	8	9	10
2	2	4	6	8	10	12	14	16	18	20
3	3	6	9	12	15	18	21	24	27	30
4	4	8	12	16	20	24	28	32	36	40
5	5	10	15	20	25	30	35	40	45	50
6	6	12	18	24	30	36	(42)	48	54	60
7	7	14	21	28	35	42	49	56	63	70
8	8	16	24	32	40	48	56	64	72	80
9	9	18	27	36	45	54	63	72	81	90
10	10	20	30	40	50	60	70	80	90	100

📄 Revise

Too tricky? If in doubt, write it out!

You can use your times tables to help you with harder mental calculations.

4 × 30 = 120 (We know that 4 × 3 = 12, so **4 × 30 = 120**)

520 × 6 = 3120 (We know that 5 × 6 = 30, so **500 × 6 = 3000**, and **20 × 6 = 120**)

123 ÷ 3 = 41 (We know that 12 ÷ 3 = 4, so **120 ÷ 3 = 40**, and **3 ÷ 3 = 1**)

2816 ÷ 4 = 704 (We know that 28 ÷ 4 = 7, so **2800 ÷ 4 = 700**, and **16 ÷ 4 = 4**)

✔ Check

1. Solve these multiplications mentally.

   a. 4 × 50 = _____

   b. 320 × 3 = _____

   c. 2 × 4444 = _____

   d. 5 × 6000 = _____

   e. 7 × 2050 = _____

2. Now try these divisions using mental methods.

   a. 300 ÷ 6 = _____

   b. 129 ÷ 3 = _____

   c. 5005 ÷ 5 = _____

   d. 3608 ÷ 4 = _____

   e. 2828 ÷ 7 = _____

⚠ Problems

Brain-buster Six people share a lottery ticket that wins £12,300. If they share the winning amount equally, how much will they each receive? _____

Square numbers and cube numbers

↺ Recap

A square number is a number multiplied by itself, for example, 2 squared is **2 × 2 = 4**

A cube number is a number multiplied by itself, and then by itself again, for example,

2 cubed is **2 × 2 × 2 = 8** (2 × 2 = 4, then 4 × 2 = 8)

2 cm
←2 cm→

2 cm
←2 cm→ 2 cm

目 Revise

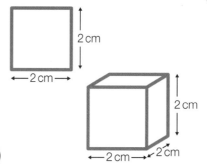

We use special numbers, called **powers**, to show square and cube numbers.

For 5 squared, instead of **5 × 5** we say **5² = 25**

For 4 cubed, instead of **4 × 4 × 4** we say **4³ = 64**

Five squared equals twenty-five.

Four cubed equals sixty-four.

✔ Check

Complete this chart, then use it to practise and learn square and cube numbers.

1	2	3	4	5	6	7	8	9	10
1²	2²								
1 × 1	2 × 2								
1	4								
1³	2³								
1 × 1 × 1	2 × 2 × 2								
1	8								

⚠ Problems

Brain-teaser Some children organise a five-a-side football match. Each player in Sanjay's team scored five goals. How many goals did his team score altogether? _____

Brain-buster A farmer stores apples in boxes. Each box holds nine layers of apples; each layer is nine apples wide and nine apples long. How many apples are there in each box?

_____

Multiplying and dividing by 10, 100 and 1000

↻ Recap

> **Please don't say *just add a zero*. That doesn't work for decimals!**

Our number system is arranged in **powers of 10.** When we multiply a number by 10 we make each digit 10 times bigger. Each digit moves one place to the left.

6 × 10 = 60   43 × 10 = 430   257 × 10 = 2570
0.4 × 10 = 4   0.07 × 10 = 0.7

When we divide a number by 10, we make each digit 10 times smaller. Each digit moves one place to the right.

6 ÷ 10 = 0.6   43 ÷ 10 = 4.3   257 ÷ 10 = 25.7
0.4 ÷ 10 = 0.04   0.07 ÷ 10 = 0.007

The decimal point doesn't move! It is always between the ones and tenths.

📋 Revise

Operation	Fact	Example 1	Example 2
× 10	Digits move one place left	65 × 10 = 650	7 × 10 = 70
× 100	Digits move two places left	65 × 100 = 6500	7 × 100 = 700
× 1000	Digits move three places left	65 × 1000 = 65,000	7 × 1000 = 7000
÷ 10	Digits move one place right	65 ÷ 10 = 6.5	7 ÷ 10 = 0.7
÷ 100	Digits move two places right	65 ÷ 100 = 0.65	7 ÷ 100 = 0.07
÷ 1000	Digits move three places right	65 ÷ 1000 = 0.065	7 ÷ 1000 = 0.007

💡 Tips

- Think about the place-value columns:

1,000,000s	100,000s	10,000s	1000s	100s	10s	1s	0.1s	0.01s	0.001s
				2	5	7			

- For any calculation, think about the number becoming bigger or smaller, moving it to the left or the right. Try this for **257 × 1000**, then for **257 ÷ 1000**. Then try some other numbers.

Talk maths

Practise using the correct vocabulary.

> 0.06 divided by 10 is 0.006. It is now 10 times smaller.

> 23 times 1000 is 23,000. It is now 1000 times bigger.

> 3 divided by 100 is 0.03. It is now 100 times smaller.

> 0.023 times 100 is 2.3. It now is 100 times bigger.

> Now, using a pencil and paper, explain to an adult or a friend how to multiply and divide by 10, 100 and 1000.

✔ Check

1. Complete these grids.

		× 10	× 100	× 1000
	3	30	300	3000
÷ 10	0.3	3		
÷ 100	0.03		3	
÷ 1000	0.003			3

		× 10	× 100	× 1000
	27			
÷ 10				
÷ 100				
÷ 1000				

		× 10	× 100	× 1000
	48			
÷ 10				
÷ 100				
÷ 1000				

		× 10	× 100	× 1000
	317			
÷ 10				
÷ 100				
÷ 1000				

⚠ Problems

Brain-teaser Tim says that an aeroplane flying over his house is 1000 times higher than the roof of his house. His house is 32 feet tall. How high up is the aeroplane?

_____

Brain-buster A new-born piglet weighs just one hundredth of its mother's weight. If its mother weighs 135.6kg, what weight will the piglet be? _____

Scaling and rates

↺ Recap

We can easily calculate fractions of quantities.

A farmer sells half his flock of 24 sheep.
$\frac{1}{2}$ of 24 sheep = 12 sheep.

Calculate **scale**: The building is 100 times bigger than the model.

The model is 20cm tall, so the building must be 2000cm, or 20 metres tall.

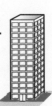

We can also calculate the rate that things happen.

If I eat 25 chips in five minutes, I have eaten five chips per minute.

🗐 Revise

Here are some problems involving scales and rates.

Examples of scales:

A child is half the height of his dad. If the child is 90cm, the father must be 180cm.

A car is four times the size of a model. If the car is 5 metres long the model must be 1.25 metres.

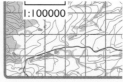
The scale of a map is 1:100,000. This means that every centimetre on the map equals a kilometre in real life.

Examples of rates:

In a traffic survey, 12 cars drive past a school in one hour. We can estimate that in six hours 72 cars will go past the school (6 × 12 = 72 cars).

A bathtub fills up at a rate of 10 litres per minute. If it takes 15 minutes to fill the bath, the bath must have a capacity of 150 litres (10 × 15 = 150 litres).

Ten people per minute go into a cinema. If it takes 40 minutes to fill all the seats, the cinema must hold 400 people (10 × 40 = 400 people).

💡 Tips

- When calculating scales, remember you can use the inverse too.
- If a road is 12km long then we know it will be 12cm on a map with a scale of 1 to 100,000.
- If a 10cm model is one fifth the size of an object, the object will be 50cm high.

Talk maths

Look at this map and check that you understand the scale. Talk about it with someone, discussing what the real-life distances will be between different features on it.

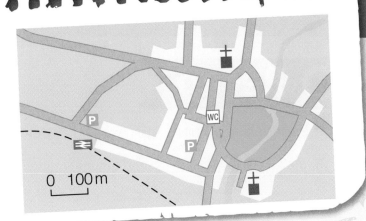

✔ Check

1. Calculate these fractions.

   a. $\frac{1}{2}$ of 6 cakes = _____

   b. $\frac{1}{4}$ of 20 adults = _____

   c. $\frac{1}{3}$ of 66 animals = _____

   d. $\frac{3}{4}$ of 100 children = _____

2. Draw two rectangles half the length and half the width of those shown.

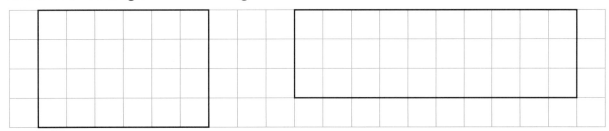

3. A teacher makes a scale model of her classroom. She builds everything at a scale of 1 to 20. Complete the chart to show the sizes of each item in her model.

Item	Room	Table	Chair	Cupboard	Waste basket
Real height	280cm	90cm	40cm	170cm	25cm
Model height					

⚠ Problems

Brain-teaser Mason measures his heart rate. It is 60 beats per minute.

How many times will his heart beat in an hour? _____

How many times in a day? _____

Brain-buster A sculptor makes a 12cm model of an athlete. The athlete is 180cm tall.

What scale is the model? (Give your answer as a fraction.) _____

Using all four operations

≠ means does <u>NOT</u> equal.

↺ Recap

Addition and multiplication work in any order, division and subtraction do not.

| $3 + 4 = 4 + 3$ | $5 \times 6 = 6 \times 5$ | $12 - 3 \neq 3 - 12$ | $10 \div 2 \neq 2 \div 10$ |

📄 Revise

Calculations and problems involving more than one operation are called **multi-step**. You must do one calculation at a time.

And you must do them in the right order!

The right order is division and multiplication first, followed by addition and subtraction, working from left to right.

Look at this calculation: $16 \div 4 + 2 \times 5 - 12$

Division first ($16 \div 4 = 4$)	$4 + 2 \times 5 - 12$
Multiplication next ($2 \times 5 = 10$)	$4 + 10 - 12$
Then addition ($4 + 10 = 14$)	$14 - 12$
And last subtraction ($14 - 12 = 2$)	**Answer** = 2

Now let's try this one: $24 - 3 \times 5 + 10 \div 2$

Multiplication first ($3 \times 5 = 15$)	$24 - 15 + 10 \div 2$
Division next ($10 \div 2 = 5$)	$24 - 15 + 5$
Then subtraction ($24 - 15 = 9$)	$9 + 5$
And last addition ($9 + 5 = 14$)	**Answer** = 14

💡 Tips

OK, everything seems to be in order here, so let's think about estimation.

- When you use maths to solve problems, think about the operations you will use, and start with an estimate. A quick estimate for $12 \times 6 - 24 \div 3 + 15$ would be to do the division and multiplication $72 - 8 + 15$ then round to get $70 - 10 + 15$, giving an estimate of 75 (the answer is 79).

💬 Talk maths

Look at these problems, which need more than one calculation. Talk about each problem with an adult or a friend, writing down the calculation and explaining why you need each operation. Then use your mental maths skills to estimate the answer before checking.

> How much would one baguette, 2 meal deals and 4 drinks cost altogether?

Baguettes	£4
Pizzas	£6
Meal deal (pizza, chips, salad)	£8
Drinks	£2

> How much change would you get from £100 if you bought 4 meal deals, 3 baguettes, 5 pizzas and 12 drinks?

> Now make up some problems of your own.

✔ Check

1. Complete these calculations.

   a. 6 × 2 − 3 = _____

   b. 6 + 2 × 3 = _____

   c. 6 ÷ 2 + 3 = _____

   d. 6 − 2 × 3 = _____

2. Mark each of these calculations right (✓) or wrong (✗).

   a. 3 × 8 + 16 ÷ 4 − 12 ÷ 6 = 26 ____

   b. 20 − 6 × 2 = 28 ____

   c. 13 − 25 ÷ 5 × 2 = 3 ____

   d. 12 − 6 + 3 = 3 ____

   e. 45 ÷ 5 + 4 × 5 − 3 × 7 = 8 ____

   f. 70 − 20 × 3 + 50 ÷ 10 = 20 ____

3. Add the missing signs to make each of these true.

   a. 5 × 5 + 12 ____ 2 − 3 × 4 = 19

   b. 12 ____ 3 ____ 14 ÷ 7 + 2 × 4 = 10

⚠ Problems

Brain-teaser A customer asks for two cabbages and five onions.

How much will this cost altogether? _____

Brain-buster A customer requests three cabbages, four onions, one lettuce and a cucumber. How much change will she receive from a £10 note?

_____

Grocer's price list

	Cabbages	80p
	Cucumbers	£1.20
	Lettuce	90p
	Onions	30p

Comparing and ordering fractions

Fractions have a numerator and a denominator.
They show us proportions of a whole.
One out of four pieces of this pizza has been eaten.

numerator —— $\dfrac{1}{4}$ —— **denominator**

We can say $\frac{1}{4}$ has been eaten…

… and $\frac{3}{4}$ has not been eaten!

Revise

We can compare and order fractions by giving them the same denominators.
To do this we must understand **equivalent fractions.**
This pizza has been cut into eight equal pieces, or eighths.

$$\frac{2}{8} = \frac{1}{4}$$

These fractions are **equivalent** because they are **the same proportion of the whole**.
We can check this by changing either one of them:

$$\frac{2 \div 2 = 1}{8 \div 2 = 4} \qquad \frac{2}{8} \qquad \frac{1 \times 2 = 2}{4 \times 2 = 8}$$

If you multiply or divide the numerator and denominator by the same number the fraction still has the same value.

To compare and order fractions, it is easier if they all have the same denominator.

Which is bigger, $\frac{1}{3}$ or $\frac{2}{5}$? We can change both fractions into fifteenths and then compare:

$$\frac{1 \times 5 = 5}{3 \times 5 = 15} \qquad \frac{2 \times 3 = 6}{5 \times 3 = 15}$$

So, $\frac{2}{5}$ is bigger than $\frac{1}{3}$. 15 is the **common denominator**.

Tips

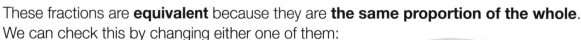

- Finding a common denominator is the same as finding a lowest common multiple.
- Remember:
  < means **is smaller than**
  > means **is bigger than**
  We can say $\frac{2}{5} > \frac{1}{3}$ and $\frac{1}{3} < \frac{2}{5}$

Talk maths

Look at the fractions in the circle and make statements using < and >.

Use these phrases to help you.

The lowest common denominator of ___ and ___ is ___

___ is bigger than ___

___ is smaller than ___

___ is equivalent to ___

> Can you make a statement that includes three fractions?

$\frac{1}{3}$ $\frac{1}{4}$

$\frac{1}{2}$ $\frac{3}{5}$ $\frac{1}{5}$

$\frac{3}{4}$ $\frac{4}{5}$

$\frac{2}{3}$ $\frac{5}{6}$ $\frac{5}{7}$

$\frac{2}{6}$ $\frac{1}{7}$

$\frac{4}{8}$ $\frac{7}{8}$

$\frac{1}{8}$ $\frac{8}{9}$

$\frac{2}{9}$ $\frac{6}{8}$ $\frac{6}{9}$

$\frac{3}{9}$

✔ Check

1. Change each fraction to give it a denominator of 8.

   a. $\frac{1}{2}$ = _____   b. $\frac{1}{4}$ = _____   c. $\frac{3}{4}$ = _____   d. 1 whole = _____

2. Change each fraction to give it a denominator of 12.

   a. $\frac{1}{2}$ = _____   b. $\frac{1}{4}$ = _____   c. $\frac{2}{3}$ = _____   d. $\frac{5}{6}$ = _____

3. True or false? Circle the correct statements.

   a. $\frac{1}{3} = \frac{2}{6}$ b. $\frac{1}{2} = \frac{3}{5}$ c. $\frac{3}{4} = \frac{6}{8}$ d. $\frac{6}{9} = \frac{2}{3}$ e. $\frac{3}{4} > \frac{2}{3}$ f. $\frac{1}{3} > \frac{2}{5}$

   g. $\frac{7}{8} > \frac{8}{10}$ h. $\frac{7}{14} > \frac{1}{2}$ i. $\frac{1}{3} < \frac{2}{6}$ j. $\frac{5}{8} < \frac{6}{7}$ k. $\frac{3}{2} < \frac{8}{10}$ i. $\frac{13}{15} < \frac{2}{3}$

4. Write the fractions in order, smallest to largest.

   a. $\frac{1}{3}, \frac{1}{5}, \frac{1}{6}, \frac{1}{2}, \frac{1}{4}, \frac{1}{10}$ _____

   b. $\frac{3}{4}, \frac{3}{5}, \frac{5}{8}$ _____

   c. $\frac{2}{3}, \frac{4}{7}, \frac{7}{9}$ _____

⚠ Problems

Brain-teaser Jen has $\frac{1}{3}$ of a pizza. Tim has $\frac{2}{5}$. Which is the larger amount? _____

Brain-buster In a football stadium, $\frac{3}{7}$ of the crowd support the blue team and $\frac{1}{3}$ support the red team. The rest don't mind who wins; they are neutral. Arrange the crowd – red, blue or neutral – in order, by fraction, starting with the smallest.

_____ < _____ < _____

Tricky fractions

↺ Recap

Fractions show proportions of a **whole**.
Equivalent fractions represent the **same** proportion.

$$\frac{3}{12} = \frac{1}{4}$$

To compare and order fractions they must have a common denominator.

Which fraction is bigger, $\frac{1}{3}$ or $\frac{1}{4}$?

$$\frac{1 \times 4 = 4}{3 \times 4 = 12}$$

$$\frac{1 \times 3 = 3}{4 \times 3 = 12}$$

$$\frac{1}{3} > \frac{1}{4}$$

3 out of 12 of the dots are red.
This is the same as one quarter.

2 out of 6 of the dots are red.
This is the same as one third.

目 Revise

There were four cakes, but someone ate half of one of them.

There are now three and a half cakes.
We write this as $3\frac{1}{2}$.
There is a whole number and a fraction. This is called a **mixed number.**

Improper fractions have a numerator that is bigger than the denominator.
Look: $\frac{7}{2}$ is an improper fraction.

Look at the cakes and think about how many halves there are.
Each whole cake has two halves, so there are seven halves altogether. $\frac{7}{2} = 3\frac{1}{2}$

$\frac{7}{2}$ is the same as saying seven divided by two ... which is three and a half!

💡 Tips

Do you know your numerators from your denominators?

- Remember that a fraction is a numerator divided by a denominator: $\frac{1}{2} = 1 \div 2$
- Converting improper fractions to mixed numbers is easy.
  $\frac{14}{3} = 14 \div 3 = 4\ r2$ and as a mixed number $= 4\frac{2}{3}$
- Practise converting improper fractions into mixed numbers by writing down some improper fractions and, with a friend, challenge each other to make them into mixed numbers.

Talk maths

Mixed numbers

Improper fractions

Each of these mixed numbers is equivalent (equal) to one of the improper fractions. Work with an adult or a friend to discuss which ones are equivalent, explaining your answers.

$3\frac{1}{4}$ $2\frac{2}{3}$ $2\frac{1}{2}$ $4\frac{1}{3}$

$3\frac{3}{5}$ $5\frac{1}{2}$ $1\frac{1}{5}$

$2\frac{3}{4}$

$2\frac{3}{10}$ $1\frac{8}{10}$ $4\frac{1}{10}$

$\frac{6}{5}$ $\frac{41}{10}$ $\frac{13}{4}$ $\frac{18}{5}$

$\frac{11}{4}$ $\frac{11}{2}$ $\frac{13}{3}$

$\frac{18}{10}$ $\frac{5}{2}$ $\frac{8}{3}$ $\frac{23}{10}$

✔ Check

1. **Change these mixed numbers to improper fractions.**

   a. $3\frac{1}{2} =$ _____

   b. $2\frac{1}{4} =$ _____

   c. $4\frac{1}{5} =$ _____

   d. $1\frac{1}{3} =$ _____

   e. $2\frac{2}{3} =$ _____

   f. $2\frac{3}{4} =$ _____

   g. $3\frac{4}{5} =$ _____

   h. $8\frac{1}{2} =$ _____

2. **Change these improper fractions to mixed numbers.**

   a. $\frac{3}{2} =$ _____

   b. $\frac{4}{3} =$ _____

   c. $\frac{5}{4} =$ _____

   d. $\frac{6}{5} =$ _____

   e. $\frac{11}{3} =$ _____

   f. $\frac{7}{4} =$ _____

   g. $\frac{15}{2} =$ _____

   h. $\frac{13}{5} =$ _____

3. **Insert =, < or > signs between each pair of fractions.**

   a. $\frac{3}{2}$ _____ $2\frac{1}{2}$

   b. $\frac{4}{3}$ _____ $1\frac{1}{3}$

   c. $\frac{7}{4}$ _____ $1\frac{1}{4}$

   d. $\frac{13}{2}$ _____ $7\frac{1}{2}$

   e. $6\frac{1}{4}$ _____ $\frac{25}{4}$

   f. $3\frac{1}{2}$ _____ $\frac{8}{2}$

   g. $\frac{10}{3}$ _____ $2\frac{2}{3}$

   h. $3\frac{1}{5}$ _____ $\frac{12}{5}$

⚠ Problems

Brain-teaser A pizza shop sells pizzas as whole pizzas and in portions of half a pizza, a third of a pizza or a quarter of a pizza.

Ali orders five pizza halves, and Joanne orders seven pizza thirds.

Who has ordered the most pizza? _____

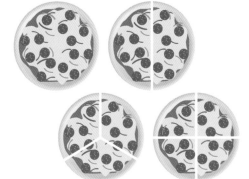

Brain-buster The pizzeria chef has made four whole pizzas. Robin orders $\frac{13}{4}$ pizzas.

How much pizza will be left over? _____

Adding and subtracting fractions

↺ Recap

We can easily compare fractions by giving them the same denominator.

$$\frac{1 \times 4 = 4}{3 \times 4 = 12}$$

$$\frac{1 \times 3 = 3}{4 \times 3 = 12}$$

so $\frac{1}{3} > \frac{1}{4}$

We can simplify fractions by dividing the top and bottom by a common factor.

$$\frac{8 \div 2 = 4}{10 \div 2 = 5}$$

$$\frac{15 \div 5 = 3}{10 \div 5 = 2} = 1\frac{1}{2}$$

Revise

To add and subtract fractions, they must have the same denominator.

Watch carefully…
To add $\frac{1}{4}$ and $\frac{3}{8}$, first find the lowest common denominator. This is 8.
Next, convert each fraction to give it a denominator of 8.

$$\frac{1 \times 2 = 2}{4 \times 2 = 8}$$

$\frac{3}{8}$ is ok

You must only add the numerators!
$\frac{3}{12} + \frac{4}{12} = \frac{7}{12}$

Then, add the new fractions:

$$\frac{2}{8} + \frac{3}{8} = \frac{5}{8}$$

Taking away is exactly the same – you only subtract the numerators.

$$\frac{7}{10} - \frac{3}{10} = \frac{4}{10}$$

💡 Tips

- When you add fractions your answer might be an improper fraction. No problem!
  For example, $\frac{2}{3} + \frac{5}{6}$

  Lowest common denominator = 6

  $\frac{2}{3} = \frac{4}{6}$ $\frac{5}{6}$ is ok $\frac{4}{6} + \frac{5}{6} = \frac{9}{6}$

  As a mixed number that is $1\frac{3}{6}$. This can be simplified to $1\frac{1}{2}$.

Talk maths

Say simple additions and subtractions of fractions with common denominators, and challenge a friend to say if you are right or wrong.

$\frac{6}{7} - \frac{5}{7} = \frac{1}{7}$ Right!

$\frac{1}{5} + \frac{2}{5} = \frac{4}{5}$ Wrong! It is $\frac{3}{5}$.

✔ Check

1. Add these fractions.

   a. $\frac{1}{5} + \frac{2}{5} =$ _____
   b. $\frac{2}{7} + \frac{3}{7} =$ _____
   c. $\frac{1}{4} + \frac{3}{4} =$ _____
   d. $\frac{3}{5} + \frac{2}{5} + \frac{1}{5} =$ _____

2. Subtract these fractions.

   a. $\frac{2}{6} - \frac{1}{6} =$ _____
   b. $\frac{5}{8} - \frac{2}{8} =$ _____
   c. $\frac{3}{4} - \frac{1}{4} =$ _____
   d. $\frac{13}{20} - \frac{7}{20} =$ _____

3. Convert and add these fractions.

   a. $\frac{1}{2} + \frac{1}{4} =$ _____
   b. $\frac{1}{2} + \frac{1}{3} =$ _____

   c. $\frac{1}{3} + \frac{1}{6} =$ _____
   d. $\frac{4}{5} + \frac{1}{6} =$ _____

4. Convert and subtract these fractions.

   a. $\frac{1}{2} - \frac{1}{4} =$ _____
   b. $\frac{1}{2} - \frac{1}{3} =$ _____

   c. $\frac{1}{3} - \frac{1}{6} =$ _____
   d. $\frac{4}{5} - \frac{1}{6} =$ _____

⚠ Problems

Brain-teaser There are two identical pizzas at a party. Jim eats $\frac{1}{6}$ of one and $\frac{1}{3}$ of the other.

How much pizza does Jim eat altogether? _____

Brain-buster Emma bakes a cake. She eats $\frac{1}{3}$ of it and her brother eats $\frac{1}{4}$ of it.

How much is left? _____

Multiplying fractions and whole numbers

↺ Recap

When multiplying by a fraction we use the word **of**.

Find $\frac{1}{2}$ of 12, $\frac{1}{4}$ of 12, $\frac{2}{3}$ of 12, $\frac{1}{6}$ of 12. Use the dots to help you.

Don't forget, multiplication works in any order. $\frac{1}{2} \times 6$ is the same as $6 \times \frac{1}{2}$.

$\frac{1}{2}$ of 12 = 6.
One quarter of 12 is 3.
$\frac{2}{3}$ of 12 is 8.
One sixth of 12 is 2.

📄 Revise

$3 \times \frac{1}{3} = 1$, because $\frac{1}{3} + \frac{1}{3} + \frac{1}{3} = \frac{3}{3}$

$5 \times \frac{1}{3} = \frac{1}{3} + \frac{1}{3} + \frac{1}{3} + \frac{1}{3} + \frac{1}{3} = \frac{5}{3}$ (or $1\frac{2}{3}$)

So, we multiply the numerator by the whole number. Look:

$$4 \times \frac{2}{3} = \frac{8}{3} \qquad 4 \times \frac{3}{5} = \frac{12}{5} \qquad 7 \times \frac{1}{2} = \frac{7}{2}$$

Can you change these into mixed numbers?

If you have to multiply a mixed number by a whole number, multiply each part separately then add them together:

$3 \times 4\frac{1}{2}$

$3 \times 4 = 12$ and $3 \times \frac{1}{2} = 1\frac{1}{2}$

So, $3 \times 4\frac{1}{2} = 12 + 1\frac{1}{2} = 13\frac{1}{2}$

When the numerator and the denominator are the same you always have one whole!

💡 Tips

Let's make sure we have mixed numbers, not mixed-up numbers!

- Keep your work neat and clear, and make your answers as simple as possible. Like this:

  What is $8 \times 2\frac{1}{5}$?

  $8 \times 2 = 16$ and $8 \times \frac{1}{5} = \frac{8}{5}$

  $8 \times 2\frac{1}{5} = 16\frac{8}{5}$ (but remember, $\frac{8}{5} = 1\frac{3}{5}$)

  So, $8 \times 2\frac{1}{5} = 17\frac{3}{5}$

Talk maths

Practise saying these calculations both ways:

$$4 \times \frac{1}{2} = \frac{4}{2} = 2$$

$$\frac{1}{2} \times 4 = 2$$

Four times one half equals four halves, which equals two.

Half of four equals two.

Now try saying these:

$$9 \times \frac{1}{3} = \frac{9}{3} = 3 \qquad \frac{1}{3} \times 9 = 3$$

Try this with some other numbers and fractions.

✔ Check

1. Complete these multiplications.

   a. $\frac{1}{2}$ of 10 = _____   **b.** $\frac{1}{4}$ of 8 = _____   **c.** $\frac{2}{3} \times 9$ = _____   **d.** $\frac{1}{2} \times 20$ = _____

2. Write the answers as mixed numbers.

   a. $10 \times \frac{1}{4}$ = _____   **b.** $3 \times \frac{1}{2}$ = _____   **c.** $4 \times \frac{3}{7}$ = _____   **d.** $20 \times \frac{1}{6}$ = _____

3. Find the answers.

   a. $2 \times 3\frac{1}{2}$ = _____   **b.** $3 \times 1\frac{1}{2}$ = _____   **c.** $2\frac{1}{6} \times 5$ = _____   **d.** $20 \times 1\frac{1}{3}$ = _____

⚠ Problems

Brain-teaser A farmer chops up trees to make logs for fires. If each tree makes $6\frac{1}{2}$ logs, how many logs will she get from three trees?

_____

Brain-buster It takes Ben $12\frac{1}{2}$ seconds to jog once around the school hall. If he keeps up a steady speed, how many laps will he complete in 100 seconds?

_____

45

Converting simple decimals and fractions

↻ Recap

A proper fraction is a proportion of one whole.

$$\frac{1}{4} \quad \frac{1}{3} \quad \frac{1}{2} \quad \frac{2}{3} \quad \frac{3}{4}$$ are all proper fractions.

Amounts less than 1 can also be represented by decimals.

0.1 is one tenth = $\frac{1}{10}$

0.2 is two tenths = $\frac{2}{10}$

0.3 is three tenths = $\frac{3}{10}$

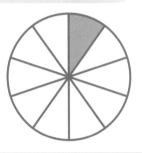

Can you keep going?

📄 Revise

Any fraction can be written as a decimal. These are common ones:

Fraction	$\frac{1}{2}$	$\frac{1}{4}$	$\frac{3}{4}$	$\frac{1}{5}$	$\frac{1}{10}$
Decimal	0.5	0.25	0.75	0.2	0.1

There are 100 dots here.

50 of them are circled in blue.
As a fraction it is $\frac{50}{100}$ or $\frac{1}{2}$.
As a decimal it is 0.5.

Any decimal can be written as a fraction. For example:

25 of the dots are circled in green.
As a fraction it is $\frac{25}{100}$ or $\frac{1}{4}$.
As a decimal this is 0.25.

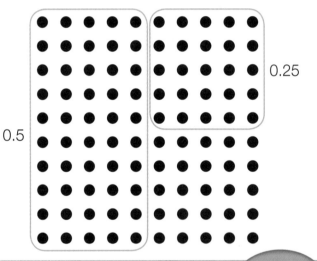

0.25

0.5

💡 Tips

Time for some decimal tips!

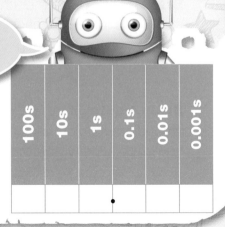

- Remember that for a decimal the first column is tenths, the second column is hundredths, and the third column is thousandths.

- We read decimals aloud using numbers zero to 10.
  We say 0.5 is **zero point five**.
  We say 0.75 is **zero point seven five**.

100s	10s	1s	0.1s	0.01s	0.001s
		•			

Talk maths

Remember to read the decimals aloud. Try other fractions too! What will $\frac{4}{5}$ be? What will $\frac{6}{10}$ be?

Use this chart to make you familiar with the decimal equivalents for these common fractions. Work with a friend and test each other.

Fraction	$\frac{1}{2}$	$\frac{1}{4}$	$\frac{3}{4}$	$\frac{1}{5}$	$\frac{1}{10}$	$\frac{1}{3}$	$\frac{2}{3}$
Decimal	0.5	0.25	0.75	0.2	0.1	0.33	0.66

✔ Check

1. Complete these charts:

a.

Fraction	$\frac{1}{10}$	$\frac{2}{10}$	$\frac{3}{10}$	$\frac{4}{10}$	$\frac{5}{10}$	$\frac{6}{10}$	$\frac{7}{10}$	$\frac{8}{10}$	$\frac{9}{10}$	$\frac{10}{10}$
Decimal	0.1	0.2								

b.

Fraction	$\frac{1}{5}$	$\frac{2}{5}$	$\frac{3}{5}$	$\frac{4}{5}$	$\frac{5}{5}$
Decimal	0.2	0.4			

2. Change these fractions to decimals.

a. $\frac{1}{2}$ = _____

b. $\frac{3}{4}$ = _____

c. $\frac{1}{10}$ = _____

3. Change these decimals to fractions.

a. 0.25 = _____

b. 0.7 = _____

c. 0.4 = _____

⚠ Problems

Brain-teaser Adjith wins a competition. As his prize he can take $\frac{3}{4}$ of a bowl of sweets, or 0.7 of the sweets. Which will give him more sweets? _____

Brain-buster A pizza is cut into four equal slices. Gemma eats one slice and says that she has eaten 0.2 of the pizza. Is she right? Explain your answer.

_____

_____

Decimal fractions

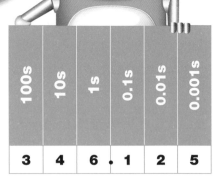

The decimal places in this place-value chart show tenths, hundredths and thousandths.

↻ Recap

Our number system uses **powers of 10**.
We sometimes call this 100s, 10s and 1s.

346 is three hundred and forty-six.
Between zero and 1 we use decimal fractions.
0.125 is **zero point one two five.**

100s	10s	1s	0.1s	0.01s	0.001s
3	4	6 .	1	2	5

📄 Revise

Can you see how many places the digit 1 moves each time?

A decimal fraction is a way of writing a fraction that has a power of 10, such as 10, 100, 1000, as its denominator.

When we divide a number by 10, 100 or 1000, we move the numbers to the right.

Fraction name	Fraction	Decimal fraction	Decimal name
one tenth	$\frac{1}{10}$	0.1	zero point one
one hundredth	$\frac{1}{100}$	0.01	zero point zero one
one thousandth	$\frac{1}{1000}$	0.001	zero point zero zero one

Here are some decimal fractions:

$$\frac{7}{10} = 0.7 \qquad \frac{31}{100} = 0.31 \qquad \frac{418}{1000} = 0.418$$

💡 Tips

- When dividing by a power of 10, move the digits one place to the right for each power of 10.

Denominator of fraction	10	100	1000
The digit 1	0.1	0.01	0.001

Talk maths

Practise using the correct words for decimal fractions and decimal places.

$\frac{45}{100}$ is *forty-five hundredths* as a fraction.

For 0.45 as a decimal fraction we say *zero point four five*.

Say these numbers as fractions and also as decimal fractions.

0.2   0.32   0.523   0.204   0.8   0.641   0.09

 **Check**

Complete this chart.

Fraction name	Fraction	Decimal fraction	Decimal name
five tenths			
twenty-three hundredths			
four hundred and thirty-five thousandths			
			zero point three
			zero point eight six
			zero point five zero seven
	$\frac{8}{10}$		
	$\frac{132}{1000}$		
		0.39	
		0.104	

⚠ Problems

Brain-teaser In a group of 100 children, 87 are right-handed. Write this number as a fraction

_____ and as a decimal _____

Brain-buster In a group of 1000 children, 235 do not like cheese. What proportion of the children do like cheese?

As a fraction _____   As a decimal _____

Numbers with three decimal places

↺ Recap

Decimal places show the decimal fraction for numbers between zero and 1.

A decimal fraction is a way of writing a fraction that has a power of 10, such as 10, 100, 1000, as its denominator.

$$\frac{123}{1000} = \mathbf{0.123}$$

1s	0.1s	0.01s	0.001s
•			

We say **one hundred and twenty-three thousandths as zero point one two three**.

📋 Revise

Say each statement aloud.

We read decimals using digit names: 0.428 is **zero point four two eight**.

Tenths are bigger than hundredths.
Hundredths are bigger than thousandths. Look:

0.6 > 0.5   0.431 > 0.429   0.1 > 0.099

0.28 < 0.3   0.739 < 0.81   0.4 < 0.515

$$\frac{1}{10} > \frac{1}{100} > \frac{1}{1000}$$

💡 Tips

Let's try to clear up different types of decimals.

- Think about what tenths, hundredths and thousands are:

  There are ten tenths in a whole.

  There are one hundred hundredths in a whole, but ten hundredths in one tenth.

  There are one thousand thousandths in a whole, but ten thousandths in one hundredth.

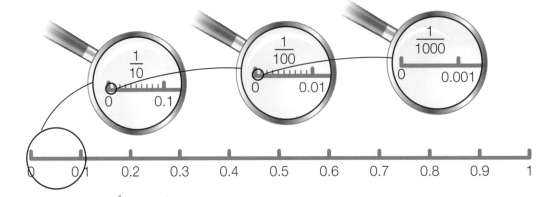

💬 Talk maths

Prepare a short presentation to explain decimal fractions to a friend or an adult you know. Explain the differences between tenths, hundredths and thousandths, and how you can write these using words, decimals or fractions.

✔ check

1. Write these in decimals using numerals.

   a. zero point four six five _____

   b. zero point two zero four _____

2. Write these in decimal fractions using numerals.

   a. six tenths _____

   b. twelve hundredths _____

   c. three hundred and twenty-five thousandths _____

3. Write these decimals in words.

   a. 0.395 _____

   b. 0.602 _____

   c. 0.005 _____

4. **a.** Arrange these decimals in order, smallest to largest.

   0.5   0.75   0.146   0.807   0.084   0.999   0.002   0.327

   _____

   b. Now position them on the number line.

   0 _____ 1

⚠ Problems

Brain-teaser Scientists can use microscopes to measure very tiny things. Circle the bugs that are less than three hundredths of a centimetre long:

Bug A: 0.101cm   Bug B: 0.029cm   Bug C: 0.009cm   Bug D: 0.031cm

Brain-buster Arrange the bugs in order, smallest to largest.

_____

Rounding decimals

⟳ Recap

Decimals are used to shows fractions of numbers. Each decimal place shows smaller and smaller parts.

Tenths   Hundredths   Thousandths

📝 Revise

We can round decimals to the nearest whole number, it's easy: 0.5 or more, round up. Less than 0.5, round down.

0.65 rounds up to 1	2.34 rounds down to 2	0.723 rounds up to 1
8.058 rounds down to 8	4.629 rounds up to 5	0.255 rounds down to 0

Sometimes we want to be more accurate, and round numbers to one decimal place.

0.65 rounds up to 0.7	2.34 rounds down to 2.3	0.723 rounds down to 0.7
8.058 rounds up to 8.1	4.629 rounds down to 4.6	0.255 rounds up to 0.3

💡 Tips

- Beware! The same number can be rounded off differently, depending on whether you round it to the nearest whole number, or to one decimal place.

	7.49	
To the nearest whole number: **7**		To the nearest tenth: **7.5**
To the nearest whole number: **8**	**7.51**	To the nearest tenth: **7.5**

Talk maths

Play *Don't Diss My Decimal*. Two or more people can play.
Take turns to think of any decimal with two or three decimal places and secretly write it down. Challenge others to ask questions about it to guess what it is. How fast can they discover your decimal?

Does it round up to the nearest whole number?

Does it round down to one decimal place?

Does it have thousandths?

✔ Check

1. Round these decimals to the nearest whole number.

   a. 0.8 _____   **b.** 1.7 _____   **c.** 4.5 _____   **d.** 0.4 _____

   e. 0.625 _____   **f.** 7.489 _____   **g.** 12.32 _____   **h.** 7.08 _____

2. Round these decimals to one decimal place.

   a. 0.83 _____   **b.** 0.77 _____   **c.** 0.45 _____   **d.** 0.838 _____

   e. 5.625 _____   **f.** 4.089 _____   **g.** 12.75 _____   **h.** 7.023 _____

3. Explain why rounding decimals is useful, but also why it might cause problems.

   _____

   _____

⚠ Problems

Brain-teaser A shopkeeper always rounds the money he makes each day to the nearest pound. Complete this chart.

Day	Monday	Tuesday	Wednesday	Thursday	Friday	Saturday
Money	£52.14	£45.61	£60.13	£46.50	£72.24	£35.51
Rounded						

Brain-buster For the week above, can you decide if the rounded amount is more or less than the money the shopkeeper actually has? Explain your answer.

_____

Simple percentages

↻ Recap

As a decimal it is 0.35: *zero point three five.*

$\frac{35}{100}$ is a fraction. We can say **35 over 100 or 35 out of 100**.

Fractions with a denominator of 100 are very important. They are also called percentages.

📝 Revise

Per cent means parts of a hundred or out of 100.

Look at the 100 grid. 65 of the 100 squares are shaded – this is 65%.

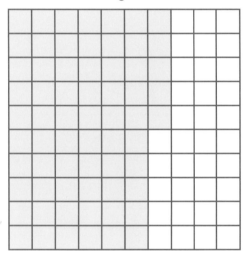

$$0.65 = \frac{65}{100} = 65\%$$

We use the words *per cent* and use the symbol % to represent it.

We can also simplify fractions as percentages:

50% = $\frac{50}{100}$ = $\frac{1}{2}$ So, 50% = $\frac{1}{2}$

💡 Tips

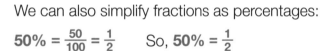

Try to learn off by heart the percentage equivalents of easy fractions.

- Because fractions can also be turned into decimal fractions, they can also be percentages. Here are some you should know:

Fraction	$\frac{1}{2}$	$\frac{1}{4}$	$\frac{1}{10}$	$\frac{2}{10}$	$\frac{1}{5}$	$\frac{2}{5}$	$\frac{65}{100}$	$\frac{3}{4}$	$\frac{1}{1}$
Decimal	0.5	0.25	0.1	0.2	0.2	0.4	0.65	0.75	1.0
Percentage	50%	25%	10%	20%	20%	40%	65%	75%	100%

 **Talk maths**

Look at the different fractions, decimals and percentages in the box.

$\frac{1}{2}$	0.1	20%	0.3	1%	$\frac{3}{4}$
67%	$\frac{1}{5}$ 0.45		1.4 100%		0.8

For each one read it aloud, then say what it would also be as a decimal, percentage or fraction.

✔ Check

1. Link the correct percentage to its equivalent fraction and decimal.

10%	0.37	$\frac{1}{2}$
25%	1.0	$\frac{1}{10}$
30%	0.1	$\frac{1}{4}$
37%	0.3	$\frac{100}{100}$
50%	0.75	$\frac{3}{10}$
60%	0.25	$\frac{3}{5}$
75%	0.5	$\frac{37}{100}$
100%	0.6	$\frac{3}{4}$

⚠ Problems

Brain-teaser There are 30 children in a class. Half of the class have school dinners and $\frac{1}{10}$ have sandwiches. The rest of the class go home for lunch.

How many children have school dinners? _____

What percentage of the class have sandwiches? _____

Brain-buster In the above class, how many children go home for lunch? _____

What percentage of the class is this? _____

Length and distance

↻ Recap

We usually measure longer distances in metres and kilometres, and shorter lengths in centimetres and millimetres.

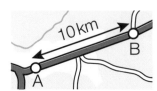 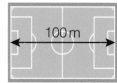 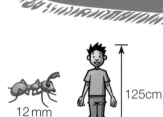

Abbreviations:
10mm = 1cm
100cm = 1m
1000m = 1km

📋 Revise

Beware: when adding lengths together they must have the same units!

We sometimes use imperial units too:

1mm = 0.1cm
1cm = 0.01m
1m = 0.001km

 TINY TOWN 5 MILES OR 8.05 KM

A six-inch ruler is around 15cm.

And a mile is around 1.61km.

💡 Tips

When measuring be sure to position the zero of your ruler properly.

- Use this guide to help you convert metric units.

Conversion	Operation	Example
mm to cm	÷ 10	12mm = 1.2cm
cm to m	÷ 100	256cm = 2.56m
m to km	÷ 1000	467m = 0.467km
cm to mm	× 10	3.5cm = 35mm
m to cm	× 100	1.85m = 185cm
km to m	× 1000	4.3km = 4300m

- For imperial units of length, just remember these two facts:
  1 inch = 2.54cm and 1 mile = 1.61km

 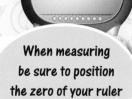

Talk maths

Can you measure to the nearest millimetre? Can you write all your measurements in millimetres?

You will need a ruler and a tape measure.

Working with an adult or a friend, choose a selection of different-sized objects. Write them in a list and then estimate their length. Write down your estimates and then swap lists. Measure the objects using the ruler and tape measure and compare answers.

✔ Check

1. Complete these conversion charts.

a.

mm	cm
10	
25	
52	
100	
	30
	17
	6
	0.2

b.

cm	m
100	
35	
450	
1000	
	80
	9
	0.9
	0.27

c.

m	km
1000	
250	
5350	
10,000	
	6
	4.5
	1.35
	0.004

2. Convert these imperial units to metric units. (Remember, 1 inch = 2.54cm and 1 mile = 1.61km.)

Imperial	Metric	Imperial	Metric	Imperial	Metric
1 inch		10 inches		100 miles	
5 inches		1 mile		300 miles	

⚠ Problems

Brain-teaser The desks in a classroom are all 120cm long. How long would a line of four desks be? Give your answer in metres. _____

Brain-buster An online map shows the length of sections of a cycle path. What is the total length of the path in km?

Path section	A–B	B–C	C–D	D–E	Total distance A–E
Distance	800m	750m	2.5km	1.3km	

Perimeter

↻ Recap

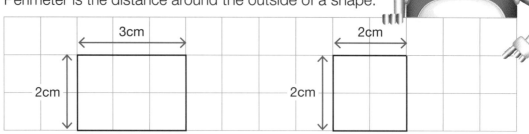

Don't forget the units!

Perimeter is the distance around the outside of a shape.

| 3cm | | 2cm |

2cm | 2cm

This rectangle has a perimeter of
3 + 3 + 2 + 2 = 10cm.
We can also say **2 × 3 + 2 × 2 = 10cm**.

This square has a perimeter
of **4 × 2 = 8cm**.

📄 Revise

If all rectangles have a length and a width, then the perimeter can be calculated with a formula. In a formula letters are used instead of numbers.

P = 2l + 2w or **P = 2(l + w)**
Perimeter = 2 × length + 2 × width
The perimeter of this rectangle is $P = 2 × 4 + 2 × 2 = 12cm$.

The formula for a square is easier, because all the **s**ides are the same length.
P = 4s
$P = 4 × 3 = 12cm$

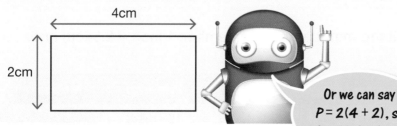

4cm

2cm

Or we can say
P = 2(4 + 2), so
P = 2 x 6 = 12cm

3cm

3cm

💡 Tips

- **Composite** shapes are made of different shapes. Be very careful how you calculate the perimeter of this shape, which was made by joing a square and a rectangle. You might have to work out some measurements!

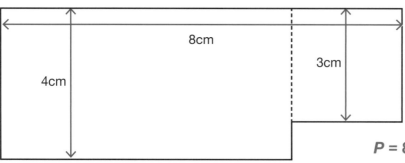

8cm

3cm

4cm

$P = 8 + 3 + 3 + 1 + 5 + 4 = 24cm$

Talk maths

Explain your answers aloud.

Practise estimating and measuring the perimeter of different rectangles and squares around your home. Try to calculate them to check your measuring.

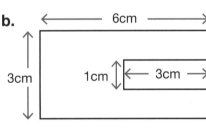

$l = 85$ cm

$w = 50$ cm

✔ check

1. Calculate the perimeter of these shapes.

   a.

   b.

   c.

   _____   _____   _____

2. Calculate the perimeter of these composite shapes.

   a.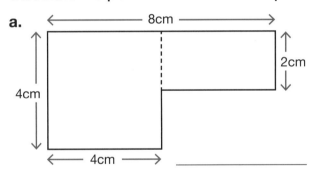

   8cm

   2cm

   4cm

   4cm _____

   b.

   6cm

   3cm

   1cm 3cm

   _____

3. Complete this chart.

Shape	Formula	Length	Width	Perimeter
Rectangle	$P =$	6mm	3mm	
Square	$P =$	2.5mm	2.5mm	

4. Find the width of each of these shapes.

   a. 6cm + 2w = 8cm, w = _____

   b. 4m + 2w = 20m, w = _____

⚠ Problems

Brain-teaser Tina's garden is 7m long and has a perimeter of 20m.

How wide is the garden? _____

Brain-buster Tables in a classroom are 1m long and 0.5m wide.

What would be the perimeter of three tables pushed end to end? _____

Area

Area is measured in **square units**.

This square is 1cm long and 1cm wide.
Its area is 1cm².

We can count squares to
calculate simple areas.

1cm

1cm

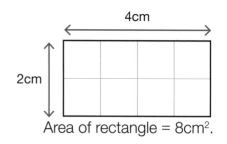

4cm

2cm

Area of rectangle = 8cm².

Revise

The formula for calculating the **A**rea of rectangles and squares is the **l**ength times the **w**idth.
A = l × w

The area of this rectangle is
A = 5 × 3 = 15cm².

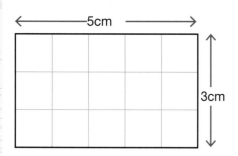

5cm

3cm

3cm

3cm

For squares, the length and the
width are the same. The area of
this square is **A = 3 × 3 = 9cm².**

This field is 40m long and 30m wide.
The area of the field is
A = 40 × 30 = 1200m².

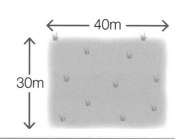

40m

30m

Don't forget
to square the
units!

Tips

- If an irregular shape is drawn on 1cm² paper we can still estimate its area.
  Just count the squares!

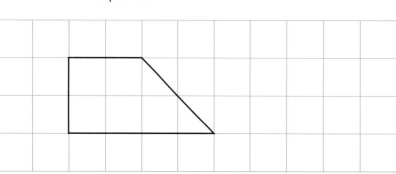

Two half
squares make one
whole cm².

💬 Talk maths

There should be more than one answer for each rectangle. How many can you find?

Look at these areas, and then tell an adult or a friend what the lengths and widths could be. Can they draw them?

Shape	Rectangle	Rectangle	Rectangle	Square	Square	Square
Area	6cm²	12cm²	30cm²	9cm²	16cm²	25cm²

✔ Check

1. **Estimate the areas of these shapes assuming each square is 1cm².**

a.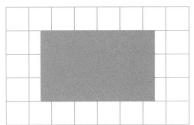

b.

c.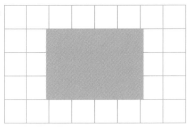

_____   _____   _____

2. **Calculate the areas of these shapes.**

   a. A rectangle with length 12cm and width 9cm. _____

   b. A square with side length 7m. _____

   c. A rectangle with length 25m and width 12m. _____

3. **Circle which shape has the larger area.**

   a. A rectangle, length 5cm and width 1cm OR a square of side 2cm?

   b. A rectangle, length 8cm and width 3cm OR a square of side 5cm?

   c. A rectangle, length 7m and width 5m OR a square of side 6m?

   d. A rectangle, length 17km and width 9km OR a square of side 12km?

⚠ Problems

Brain-teaser Annie's garden is 3m long and 5m wide. It was all grass but Annie has cut a square flowerbed, with side length of 1m, in the centre. What area of grass is left? _____

Brain-buster A farmer plants nine potatoes in every square metre of earth.

How many potatoes will she grow in a field 120m long and 75m wide? _____

Mass, capacity and volume

↻ Recap

Mass is sometimes measured in pounds and ounces.

2lb

Capacity is sometimes measured in pints and fluid ounces.

📄 Revise

Maybe that's why they're called cube numbers!

We measure volume in **cubic centimetres** or **cubic metres**.
The **V**olume of this cube is
$V = 1 \times 1 \times 1 = 1\text{cm}^3$.

1cm

1cm

1cm

When we add masses together, the units must be the same.

 **50kg**
50 kg

 12kg
12kg

=  **62kg**

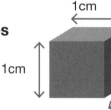
1000 l
900
800
700
600
500
400
300
200
100

+

500 ml
400
300
200
100

=

1500 ml
1500
1000
500

1500ml

It's the same with capacity.

💡 Tips

Let's make sure we know our units.

- Essential units for you to know:

Mass	1000g = 1kg
Capacity	1000ml = 1l

- To convert millilitres to litres, and to convert grams to kilograms, divide by 1000.
- To convert litres to millilitres, and kilograms to grams, multiply by 1000.

Talk maths

Volume is the amount of space an object takes up. Capacity is used to talk about how much something can hold.

Volume and capacity are have similarities.

Volume is usually measured in cubic units, such as cm³.
One cubic centimetre equals one millilitre.

Collect some small objects from around your home, and work with an adult to try and estimate their volume. It would be great if you could use 1cm cubes to help you, but it is ok just to estimate.

✔ Check

1. Convert these masses.

Object	Grams	Kilograms
Child		50kg
Dog		12kg
Pencil	75g	
Book	408g	

2. Convert these capacities.

Object	Millilitres	Litres
Teapot		1.25l
Sink		8.5l
Mug	125ml	
Thimble	12ml	

3. Use the completed tables to answer these questions.

    a. What is the mass of a pencil and a book? _____

    b. What is the capacity of a mug and a thimble? _____

    c. What is the mass of a child and a book? _____

    d. What is the capacity of a teapot and a thimble? _____

⚠ Problems

Brain-teaser Hakan weighs 50kg and Aysha weighs 35kg. Their teacher weighs 65kg.
How much extra weight would their teacher need to add to make a seesaw balance if he sits on one end and the children on the other?

Brain-buster Françoise has a litre bottle of water. How much will she have left if she fills two thimbles and a mug? The capacity of one thimble is 12ml and of one mug is 125ml.

_____

Time

Seconds, **minutes**, **hours**, **days**, **weeks**, and **years** – these are all units of time. Months are a bit different because they are not all the same length.

60 seconds = 1 minute
60 minutes = 1 hour
24 hours = 1 day
7 days = 1 week
365 days = 1 year

> Except for leap years – they have an extra day!

Analogue clocks show 12-hour time.
Digital clocks can show **12-hour** or **24-hour time**.

🗒 Revise

Converting between different units of time is not difficult.

Minutes to seconds	× 60		Seconds to minutes	÷ 60
Hours to minutes	× 60		Minutes to hours	÷ 60
Days to hours	× 24		Hours to days	÷ 24
Weeks to days	× 7		Days to weeks	÷ 7
Years to days	× 365		Days to years	÷ 365

Remainders stay in the same units.
For example, change 400 days to years.
400 ÷ 365 = 1 remainder 35
So, **400 days = 1 year and 35 days**.

> Or one year and five weeks. Can you see that?

💡 Tips

- Be careful adding minutes that move on to a new hour. For example, if a school's lunch break starts at 12:30pm and lasts for 40 minutes, at what time will the break be over? There are 60 minutes in an hour, so 12:30pm + 40 = 1:10pm.

- If you are not sure, use a clock or watch to help you.

- Also, be aware of the 12-hour and 24-hour clocks. Remember that 1pm = 13:00, 6pm = 18:00, and so on.

Talk maths

Talk to as many people as you can about their birthday. Try to find out what time of day they were born.

Use a calendar to challenge your friends to work out how many days there are between their birthday and yours.

Look at timetables at bus stops or train stations. Can you find out how long different journeys take?

DID YOU KNOW?

10 years is known as a decade, 100 years is known as a century and 1000 years is known as a millennium.

✔ Check

1. Complete this chart to convert 12-hour clock times to 24-hour clock times.

12-hour	Midnight	2.10am	9.15am	Noon	3.30pm	9pm	11.59pm
24-hour							

2. Write these times in the unit shown.

   a. 3 hours in minutes _____   b. 2 days in hours _____

   c. 12 weeks in days _____   d. 4 years in days _____

   e. 100 minutes in hours _____   f. 100 hours in days _____

   g. 225 minutes in hours _____   h. 500 days in years _____

3. Add these times.

   a. 8 hours and 25 minutes + 3 hours and 30 minutes _____

   b. 1 day 7 hours and 25 minutes + 3 days 5 hours and 16 minutes _____

   c. 2 days 17 hours and 45 minutes + 6 days 9 hours and 13 minutes _____

⚠ Problems

Brain-teaser Rob's school bus journey takes 17 minutes. If he gets on the bus at 8:20am, what time will he arrive at school?

_____

Brain-buster Gayle's new baby brother will be exactly one week old at 6pm today. Help Gayle to calculate how many seconds old her new brother will be at 6pm.

_____

Money

↻ Recap

Money shows us the cost of things.
We use pounds (£) and pence (p).

£1 = 100p

We show pence using decimals.

13 pounds and 65 pence = £13.65

> If you use the £ sign you don't need to add a p at the end.

📋 Revise

You can use all your number skills to solve money problems.

> Converting pounds to pence? × 100
> Converting pence to pounds? ÷ 100

	Example	Try these:
Addition	£13.50 + £6.37 = £19.87	£7.32 + £2.50 =
Subtraction	£20.00 − £16.25 = £3.75	£10.00 − £8.85 =
Multiplication	£2.30 × 4 = £9.20	£5.25 × 5 =
Division	£9.00 ÷ 4 = £2.25	£4.50 ÷ 3 =
Fractions	$\frac{1}{2}$ of £16.50 = £8.25	$\frac{1}{4}$ of £20 =

💡 Tips

- Calculations with money are just the same as using any decimals that have two decimal places.

£47.87 + £38.17

```
  4 7 . 8 7
+ 3 8 . 1 7
-----------
  8 6 . 0 4
  |   |   |
```

Answer: **£86.04**

> Not sure about money? Maybe decimals can help.

💬 Talk maths

Work with an adult or a friend. Use these items to create multi-step problems to challenge each other. Use written methods to calculate answers if you need to, but be sure to discuss your answers.

Example: If I buy two apples and a banana, how much change will I get from a £2 coin?

2 × 23 + 35 = 81p

2.00 − 0.81 = £1.19

(Price tags: 23p, 52p, 35p, £1.80p, 90p, £1.10p, £2.20p, £4.90)

✔ Check

1. Convert these pence to pounds.

Pence	200p	135p	6325p	9p	10,903p
Pounds					

2. Convert these pounds to pence.

Pounds	£4	£2.56	£0.12	£82	£403.20
Pence					

3. Complete these calculations (use written methods if necessary).

a. £4.52 + £3.25 = _____

b. £12.35 + £9.80 = _____

c. £10.00 − £8.30 = _____

d. £45.45 − £3.72 = _____

e. £3.35 × 2 = _____

f. £14.08 × 5 = _____

g. £50.00 ÷ 4 = _____

h. $\frac{1}{2}$ of £15.40 = _____

⚠ Problems

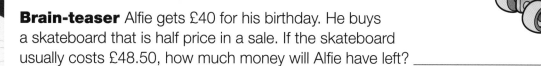

Brain-teaser Alfie gets £40 for his birthday. He buys a skateboard that is half price in a sale. If the skateboard usually costs £48.50, how much money will Alfie have left? _____

Brain-buster A head teacher orders ten desks that cost £35.50 each and 20 chairs for £12.25 each. What will be the total cost? _____

Angle facts

↻ Recap

We measure angles with a protractor.

📝 Revise

A right angle is 90°	A straight line is 180°
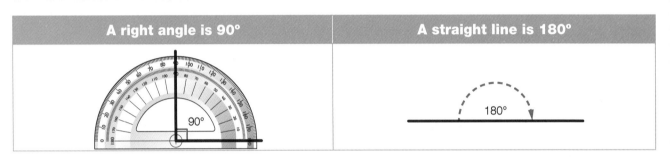	

Acute angles are between 0° and 90°	Obtuse angles are between 90° and 180°

50°

160°

Angles greater than 180° are called *reflex* angles	A complete turn is 360°
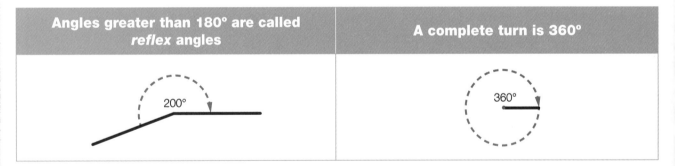	

200°

360°

💡 Tips

Stuck? Let's come at things from a different angle.

- Make sure you can use a protractor properly. Check the size of each of the angles on this page.

- Think about it… two lines that make an acute angle on the inside will make a reflex angle on the outside. These two angles add up to 360°.

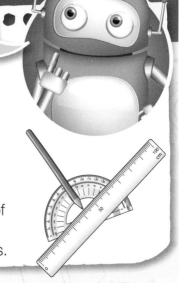

> How accurate were your angle estimates?

Talk maths

You will need paper, a pencil, a ruler and a protractor.

First, explain to an adult how to use a protractor properly. Demonstrate the correct way to place it on an angle, and how to measure the angle using the correct readings.

Next, work together to become angle experts: draw a selection of angles and then estimate their size.

Finally, measure each one and compare them with your estimates.

✔ Check

1. Measure these angles. Write down their size and their name, such as *acute*.

a.

size _____

name _____

b.

size _____

name _____

c.

size _____

name _____

2. Draw these angles, and then name them.

a. 90°

name _____

b. 300°

name _____

c. 15°

name _____

⚠ Problems

Brain-teaser Aaron only has a ruler and a pencil, but he can still say if an angle is acute, obtuse or reflex. How can he do this?

_____

Brain-buster Amy draws a straight line and then draws another line to its middle to make two separate angles. She measures the acute angle to be 42°. She says that the obtuse angle must be 138°. Explain why she is right.

_____

Rotating angles

$90° + 90° = 180°$

↻ Recap

A right angle is 90°.
Two right angles make 180°.

90°

90°
90°

📋 Revise

There are 360° in a complete rotation.

A complete rotation is four right angles.
$90° + 90° + 90° + 90° = 360°$

Each rotation of 90° is a right angle.

Rip the four corners off a piece of A5
paper and put them together. What do you notice?

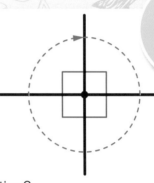

Imagine standing
at the centre of this
circle and turning ninety
degrees four times.

💡 Tips

- You can rotate clockwise or anticlockwise.

Use clocks to practise counting in right
angles. This clock shows a clockwise
rotation of 270°.

If you go anticlockwise the rotation is 90°.

270 + 90 = 360° (one complete turn)

Compasses have a 90° rotation
between each point. North to east is 90°
clockwise, or 270° anticlockwise.

North to south is 180° clockwise and
180° anticlockwise!

 **Talk maths**

You can play a mini version of this activity using an action figure on paper!

You will need some chalk and a flat area of ground.

With a friend, find a safe and quiet place, and then use chalk to draw a large cross on the ground and mark the end of each line 1, 2, 3, 4.

Challenge each other to rotate the correct number of right angles. For example, *face number 2 and then rotate 90°*. Which number are you facing now?

 **Check**

1. **Draw these angles using a protractor.**

   a. 90° **b.** 180° **c.** 270°

   d. 360° **e.** 0°

⚠ Problems

Brain-teaser To get from midday to 9pm, how many right angles does the hour hand on a clock have to turn through? _____

How many degrees is this? _____

Brain-buster Michael stands facing south. He rotates 270° clockwise, and then he turns an amount. If he finishes facing west, how many degrees did he turn the second time, and in what direction? _____

2D shapes

Each of the angles in a square is 90°. A circle has one side and no corners!

⟳ Recap

We say that different 2D shapes have different properties.

Triangle	Quadrilateral	Pentagon	Hexagon	Heptagon	Octagon
3 sides	4 sides	5 sides	6 sides	7 sides	8 sides

All of these shapes are **regular** – all the sides are the same length, and in each shape all of the angles are the same size.

Revise

Irregular shapes have the same number of sides and angles as their corresponding regular shapes, but the sides and angles are not identical.

Triangle	Quadrilateral	Pentagon	Hexagon	Heptagon	Octagon
3 sides	4 sides	5 sides	6 sides	7 sides	8 sides

Tips

- There are several types of quadrilateral that you also need to know about.

Square	Rectangle	Rhombus	Parallelogram	Kite	Trapezium
All sides equal, all angles 90°	Opposite sides equal, all angles 90°	All sides equal, opposite angles equal	Opposite sides equal, and parallel opposite angles equal	Adjacent sides equal	Only one pair of parallel sides

- **Adjacent** means next to.

 **Talk maths**

Cover the names of the shapes on the opposite page. Try to identify each shape, telling a friend or an adult why you think it is that particular shape.
Then cover the shapes and try to describe the properties for each name.

✔ Check

1. Name each shape, and say if it is regular or irregular.

a.

b.

c.

d.

_____   _____   _____   _____

_____   _____   _____   _____

2. Explain why a rectangle is not a regular quadrilateral.

_____

_____

3. Label these quadrilaterals.

a. _____   b. _____   c. _____

d. _____   e. _____   f. _____

⚠ Problems

Brain-teaser Write the length of the missing sides and the size of the missing angles on this rectangle.

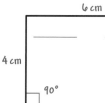

6 cm

4 cm

90°

3D shapes

↻ Recap

3D shapes have faces, edges and vertices.

A corner is a **vertex**.
The plural is **vertices**.

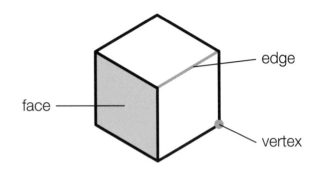

edge

face

vertex

📋 Revise

Irregular shapes have the same number of sides and angles as their corresponding regular shapes, but the sides and angles are not identical.

Shape						
Name	Cube	Cuboid	Cone	Sphere	Cylinder	Triangular prism
Faces	6	6	2	1	3	5
Edges	12	12	1	0	2	9
Vertices	8	8	0	0	0	6

💡 Tips

- Drawing shapes to look 3D is called isometric drawing.
- The trick is to draw one end face, and then draw the edges as parallel lines.

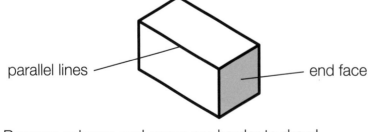

parallel lines

end face

- Beware: spheres and cones are harder to draw!

Talk maths

With two or more people, play the *Yes/No* game for shapes.
Choose a person to be the drawer.
All other players will be the guessers.
The drawer draws a shape on paper, making sure the guessers don't see it.
The guessers then ask questions to find out which shape has been drawn.
The only answer the drawer can give is *yes* or *no*.

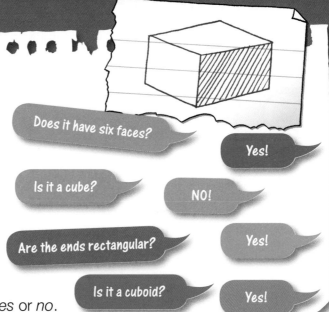

Does it have six faces? Yes!

Is it a cube? NO!

Are the ends rectangular? Yes!

Is it a cuboid? Yes!

✔ Check

1. Use a pencil and ruler to draw each of these shapes.

triangular prism	cylinder	cube	cuboid

2. Name the shapes from their descriptions below.

a. I have only one face. _____

b. I have six identical faces. _____

c. I have only one edge. _____

d. I have three faces. _____

e. I have five faces. _____

f. I have six faces, some different. _____

⚠ Problems

Brain-teaser Sanjay draws a 3D shape with a square end; each edge of the square is 4cm. The other sides of his shape are 6cm long. What shape has he drawn?

_____

Brain-buster A cone and a cylinder are both 10cm long and both have a base with a diameter of 5cm. If they were hollow, which one could hold more water? Explain your answer.

_____

_____

Reflecting and translating shapes

↺ Recap

We draw a grid with an *x*-axis and a *y*-axis, and we can plot the corners of polygons (2D shapes).

Points on the grid are shown with the *x*-coordinate first, and then the *y*-coordinate.

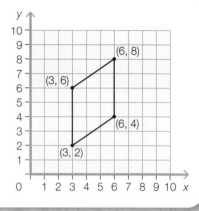

Remember, along first, then up.

▤ Revise

A has been reflected to A¹.
The *x*-coordinate has not changed.

We can also reflect shapes.
Try reflecting the triangle.

We can also **translate** shapes.

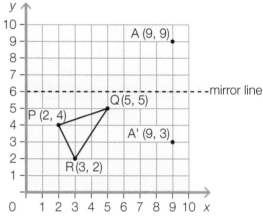

That is when all the points move the same distance.

The square has been translated (5, 4).

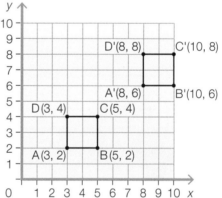

💡 Tips

- **Reflections:**
  In a vertical mirror line, only the *x*-coordinates change.
  In a horizontal mirror line, only the *y*-coordinates change.

- **Translations:**
  All the *x*-coordinates should change by the same amount.
  And so should the *y*-coordinates.

Talk maths

Take turns to choose a point on the graph and say its coordinates. Challenge someone to reflect or translate it.

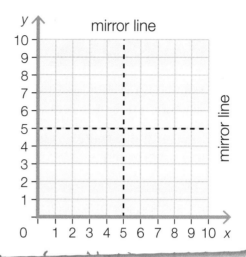

Reflect the point (2, 3) vertically.

Reflect the point (9, 1) horizontally.

Translate the point (0, 5) by (2, 3).

Translate the point (4, 4) by (−2, −3).

✔ Check

1. Look at the graph below. Using squared paper:

   a. Reflect the square PQRS.

   b. Write the coordinates of the new square.

   c. Plot a triangle ABC: A (6, 5), B (9 ,6), C (7, 9).

   d. Reflect the triangle.

2. Look at the graph below. Using squared paper:

   a. Translate the square WXYZ by (3, 2).

   b. Write the coordinates of the new square.

   c. Plot a triangle DEF: D (2, 7), E (4, 9), F (3, 5).

   d. Translate it by (5, −4).

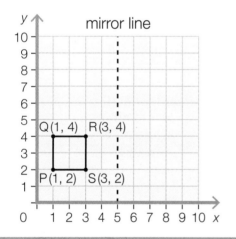

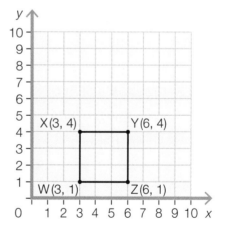

⚠ Problems

Brain-buster Gayle has worked out a method for calculating the coordinates of reflected shapes without drawing them. Explain her method.

_____

_____

Line graphs

↺ Recap

We can represent information and data in different types of charts and graphs.

Each of these graphs has a vertical *y*-axis and a horizontal *x*-axis.

Bar charts and pictograms are useful for presenting information from surveys, such as:

- How do you travel to school?
- What is your favourite snack?
- Do you have any pets?

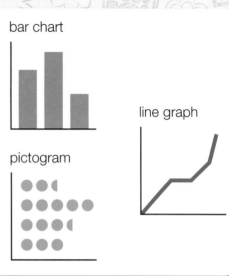

bar chart

line graph

pictogram

📄 Revise

Line graphs are useful to show how things change over time, such as temperature, growth and speed.

This graph shows the time taken for an 8km cycle ride.

Find these bits of information on the graph:

- The journey starts at 1pm.
- After 20 minutes the cyclist stops for five minutes.
- The cyclist travels fastest from 25 minutes to 40 minutes.
- The cyclist stops again after 40 minutes.
- The journey finishes at 8km.

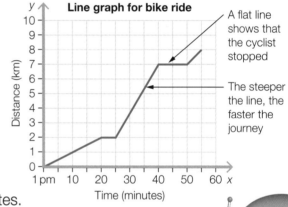

Line graph for bike ride

A flat line shows that the cyclist stopped

The steeper the line, the faster the journey

Look carefully at the scale on each axis.

💡 Tips

When it comes to tips on graphs, I draw the line!

- Line graphs can be used to estimate information.
- This graph shows the height a tree grew every two years for ten years.
- We can draw lines to show its height after three years.

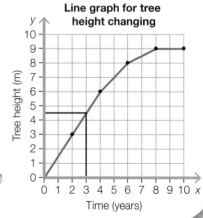

Line graph for tree height changing

 **Talk maths**

This line graph shows the distance travelled by a lorry on a long journey.

Look at the graph with an adult and talk about what each part means.

What is each axis for?

What is the scale for each axis?

How long is the journey?

What is happening when the line is flat?

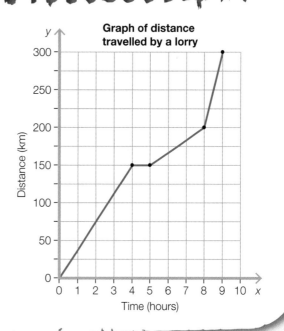

Graph of distance travelled by a lorry

✔ Check

1. Philip grows a plant at home. He measures it at the end of each week and records its height in a chart.

Time (weeks)	1	2	3	4	5	6	7	8	9	10
Height (cm)	0	1	3	5	7	10	11	12	12	12

a. Draw a line graph to show how the plant has grown.

b. When was the plant 3cm high? _____

c. When did the plant stop growing? _____

d. Which week did the plant grow the most?

_____

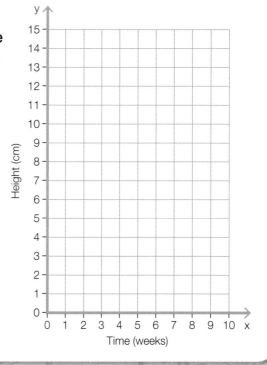

⚠ Problems

Brain-teaser What is the highest temperature?

_____

When was temperature highest? _____

Brain-buster Find the difference between the highest and lowest temperatures.

_____

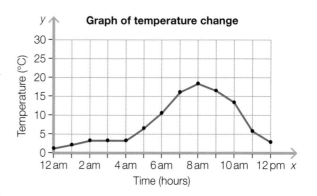

Graph of temperature change

Tables and timetables

You can spot facts about planets and compare them too. Each column has different units.

↻ Recap

Information is often presented in tables. This table provides complicated information about some planets in our solar system.

Planet	Diameter (km)	Day length (hours)	Orbit time (days)	Temp. (°C)
Mercury	4878	4223	88	167
Venus	12,104	2808	225	480
Earth	12,756	24	365	20
Mars	6794	24.5	687	−65

📄 Revise

This timetable shows bus times from the bus station to the local school.

Check with an adult that you know how to read the timetable properly. These buses have a circular route. Can you see the halfway point?

Can you see the difference between the number 6 and 7 bus routes? Why wouldn't you go to the supermarket on the number 6 bus? What is the longest time it takes to get between two stops?

BUS TIMETABLE

Bus number	6	7	6	7	6	7
Bus station	10:00	10:15	10:30	10:45		
High Street	10:08	10:23	10:38	10:53		
Supermarket		10:30		11:00		
Train station	10:15		10:45			
Doctor's surgery	10:24	10:34	10:54	11:04		
School	10:27	10:37	10:57	11:07		
Doctor's surgery	10:30	10:40	11:00	11:10		
Train station	10:39		11:09			
Supermarket		10:45		11:15		
High street	10:46	10:52	11:16	11:22		
Bus station	10:54	11:00	11:24	11:30		

Can you spot the patterns for the bus times? Try filling in the last two columns.

💡 Tips

Let your fingers do the walking!

- Use your fingers to help you trace along timetables and charts. Or if you have a ruler available, using this even better – it is easy to misread timetables and charts.

💬 Talk maths

Ask an adult to provide you with a timetable. These are usually available for local buses and trains. You can get them from the station and they will probably be available online.

Use the timetables to plan a day trip.
Can you plan at least four journeys with as little time waiting as possible?

DID YOU KNOW?

There are over 5 billion bus journeys made in the UK each year.

✔ Check

1. **Use the table on page 80 to answer these questions about our solar system.**

   a. Which is the largest planet? _____

   b. Which is the coldest planet? _____

   c. Which planet has the fastest orbit? _____

   d. Which planets have a similar length of day? _____
   _____

2. **Use the bus timetable on page 80 to answer these questions.**

   a. Which bus has a shorter journey from the bus station to the school? _____

   b. How often does the number 6 leave the bus station? _____

   c. How long is the journey from the doctor's surgery to the school? _____

   d. Why do you think the number 6 round journey takes longer? _____
   _____

⚠ Problems

Look at the bus timetable on page 80.

Brain-teaser Trevor has a doctor's appointment at 10:45am.

Which bus should he catch from the bus station? _____

Brain-buster A number 7 bus arrives at school at 15:07.

What time did it leave the bus station? _____

Answers: Year 5

NUMBER AND PLACE VALUE

Page 9

Check

1 thirty-four thousand eight hundred and five

2 237,120

3 forty thousand or four ten thousands

4 7, 12, 725, 25,612, 50,000, 225,421, 899,372, 1,000,000

5 **a.** 3521 < 5630   **b.** 15,204 > 9798
   c. 833,521 > 795,732

Brain-teaser Winchcomb City
Brain-buster Winchcomb City, Fintan United, Forest Rovers

Page 11

Check

1 124, 224, 324, 424, 524, 624

2 12,906, 11,906, 10,906, 9906, 8906, 7906

3 320,435, 420,435, 520,435, 620,435, 720,435, 820,435

4 243,000, 233,000, 223,000, 213,000, 203,000, 193,000

Brain-teaser 13 months
Brain-buster 73,456

Page 13

Check

1 **a.** 0   **b.** 0   **c.** –9   **d.** –4

2 –6, –4, –2, 0, 2, 4, 6

3 **a.** –   **b.** +   **c.** +   **d.** –

4 **a.** 4   **b.** 3   **c.** 9   **d.** 2

Brain-teaser –2°C
Brain-buster 36°C

Page 15

Check

	nearest 10	nearest 100	nearest 1000	nearest 10,000	nearest 100,000
67	70	100	0	0	0
145	150	100	0	0	0
3320	3320	3300	3000	0	0
78,249	78,250	78,200	78,000	80,000	100,000
381,082	381,080	381,100	381,000	380,000	400,000
555,555	555,560	555,600	556,000	560,000	600,000

Brain-teaser 50,000
Brain-buster Loss on a bad match: £46,000; Gain on a good match: £54,000

Page 16

Check

1 **a.** 8   **b.** 23   **c.** 300   **d.** 95   **e.** 104   **f.** 140   **g.** 610
   h. 900

2 **a.** XXII   **b.** XLI   **c.** LV   **d.** XCIII   **e.** CXII   **f.** CLX
   g. CCXII   **h.** CMLXV

3 320,435, 420,435, 520,435, 620,435, 720,435, 820,435

4 243,000, 233,000, 223,000, 213,000, 203,000, 193,000

Brainbuster Date: CDX   Years in Britain: CDLXV

CALCULATIONS

Page 17

Check

1 **a.** 96   **b.** 226   **c.** 5276   **d.** 19,954   **e.** 130,320

2 **a.** 34   **b.** 95   **c.** 246   **d.** 1500   **e.** 265,675

Brain-teaser 273
Brain-buster £1097

Page 19

Check

1 **a.** 3244   **b.** 12,309   **c.** 70,180   **d.** 621,229

2 **a.** 5966   **b.** 69,636   **c.** 213,925   **d.** 658,930

Brain-teaser Yes
Brain-buster No

Page 21

Check

1 **a.** 139   **b.** 4163   **c.** 189,419

2 **a.** 119   **b.** 2273   **c.** 3968   **d.** 3861   **e.** 116,923

Brain-teaser Bim and Bom
Brain-buster 212,980

Page 23

Check

1 1, 2, 3, 6

2 4, 8, 12, 16, 20, and so on.

3 **a.** 1 × 15 and 3 × 5   **b.** 1 × 27 and 3 × 9
   c. 1 × 24, 2 × 12, 3 × 8 and 4 × 6
   d. 1 × 30, 2 × 15, 3 × 10 and 5 × 6.

4 **a.** 1, 2 and 4   **b.** 1 and 5   **c.** 1, 2 and 4
   d. 1, 2, 5, 10, 25 and 50

Brain-teaser

Children	1	2	3	4	6	8	12	24
Chocolates	24	12	8	6	4	3	2	1

Shared between 5 children there would be 4 chocolates left over.
Brain-buster No, because 7 is not a factor of 365,
52 × 7 = 364

Page 25

Check

1 A number that can only be divided by itself and 1.

2 2, 3, 5, 7, 11, 13, 17, 19

3 **a.** 25 is not a prime because 5 is a factor   **b.** 71 is a prime because it can only be divided by itself and 1   **c.** 87 is not a prime because 3 and 29 are factors

4 Many possible answers, such as 101, 103, 107, 109, 113

Brain-teaser No, because it can be divided by 7 and 11.
Brain-buster 27 is not a prime number because it can be divided by 3 and 9.

Page 27

Check

1 **a.** 273   **b.** 552   **c.** 1395   **d.** 3528

2 **a.** 315   **b.** 832   **c.** 795   **d.** 1320

Brain-teaser £6.45
Brain-buster Yes, because 475 × £13 = £6175

Page 29

Check

1   **a.** 19   **b.** 11r2   **c.** 46r4   **d.** 32r2

2   **a.** 14   **b.** 25   **c.** 65r2   **d.** 21r3

Brain-teaser 12 times
Brain-buster 11 pieces per child. Teacher has 15 pieces.

Page 30

Check

1   **a.** 200   **b.** 960   **c.** 8888   **d.** 30,000   **e.** 14,350

2   **a.** 50   **b.** 43   **c.** 1001   **d.** 902   **e.** 404

Brain-buster £2050 each

Page 31

Check

1

1	2	3	4	5	6	7	8	9	10
1^2	2^2	3^2	4^2	5^2	6^2	7^2	8^2	9^2	10^2
1×1	2×2	3×3	4×4	5×5	6×6	7×7	8×8	9×9	10×10
1	4	9	16	25	36	49	64	81	100
1^3	2^3	3^3	4^3	5^3	6^3	7^3	8^3	9^3	10^3
1×1×1	2×2×2	3×3×3	4×4×4	5×5×5	6×6×6	7×7×7	8×8×8	9×9×9	10×10×10
1	8	27	64	125	216	343	512	729	1000

Brain-teaser 25 goals
Brain-buster 9 × 9 × 9 = 729 apples

Page 33

Check

1

	×10	×100	×1000
	3	30	300	3000
÷10	0.3	3	30	300
÷100	0.03	0.3	3	30
÷1000	0.003	0.03	0.3	3

	×10	×100	×1000
	27	270	2700	27000
÷10	2.7	27	270	2700
÷100	0.27	2.7	27	270
÷1000	0.027	0.27	2.7	27

	×10	×100	×1000
	48	480	4800	48000
÷10	4.8	48	480	4800
÷100	0.48	4.8	48	480
÷1000	0.048	0.48	4.8	48

	×10	×100	×1000
	317	3170	31700	317000
÷10	31.7	317	3170	31700
÷100	3.17	31.7	317	3170
÷1000	0.317	3.17	31.7	317

Brain-teaser 32,000 feet
Brain-buster 1.356kg

Page 35

Check

1   **a.** 3 cakes   **b.** 5 adults   **c.** 22 animals   **d.** 75 children

2   Children's drawing of:
     a rectangle 3 squares wide and 2 deep
     a rectangle 5 squares wide and 1 and a half squares deep

3

Item	Room	Table	Chair	Cupboard	Basket
Real height	280cm	90cm	40cm	170cm	25cm
Model height	14cm	4.5cm	2cm	8.5cm	1.25cm

Brain-teaser 3600 beats in an hour; 86,400 beats in a day
Brain-buster Model scale: $\frac{1}{15}$

Page 37

Check

1   **a.** 9   **b.** 12   **c.** 6   **d.** 0

2   **a.** correct   **b.** wrong (8)   **c.** correct   **d.** wrong (9)
     e. correct   **f.** wrong (5)

3   **a.** ÷   **b.** ÷ and −

Brain-teaser £3.10
Brain-buster £4.30

FRACTIONS, DECIMALS AND PERCENTAGES

Page 39

Check

1   **a.** $\frac{4}{8}$ **b.** $\frac{2}{8}$ **c.** $\frac{6}{8}$ **d.** $\frac{8}{8}$

2   **a.** $\frac{6}{12}$ **b.** $\frac{3}{12}$ **c.** $\frac{8}{12}$ **d.** $\frac{10}{12}$

3   **a.** True   **b.** False   **c.** True   **d.** True   **e.** True   **f.** False
     g. True   **h.** False   **i.** False   **j.** True   **k.** True   **l.** False

4   **a.** $\frac{1}{10}, \frac{1}{6}, \frac{1}{5}, \frac{1}{4}, \frac{1}{3}, \frac{1}{2}$ **b.** $\frac{3}{5}, \frac{5}{8}, \frac{3}{4}$ **c.** $\frac{4}{7}, \frac{2}{3}, \frac{7}{9}$

Brain-teaser $\frac{2}{5}$
Brain-buster neutral ($\frac{5}{21}$) < red ($\frac{7}{21}$) < blue ($\frac{9}{21}$) **or**
neutral ($\frac{5}{21}$) < red ($\frac{1}{3}$) < blue ($\frac{3}{7}$)

Page 41

Check

1   **a.** $\frac{7}{2}$ **b.** $\frac{9}{4}$ **c.** $\frac{21}{5}$ **d.** $\frac{4}{3}$ **e.** $\frac{8}{3}$ **f.** $\frac{11}{4}$ **g.** $\frac{19}{5}$ **h.** $\frac{17}{2}$

2   **a.** $1\frac{1}{2}$ **b.** $1\frac{1}{3}$ **c.** $1\frac{1}{4}$ **d.** $1\frac{1}{5}$ **e.** $3\frac{2}{3}$ **f.** $1\frac{3}{4}$ **g.** $7\frac{1}{2}$ **h.** $2\frac{3}{5}$

3   **a.** $\frac{3}{2} < 2\frac{1}{2}$ **b.** $\frac{4}{3} = 1\frac{1}{3}$ **c.** $\frac{7}{4} > 1\frac{1}{4}$ **d.** $\frac{13}{2} < 7\frac{1}{2}$
     e. $6\frac{1}{4} = \frac{25}{4}$ **f.** $3\frac{1}{2} < \frac{8}{2}$ **g.** $\frac{10}{3} > 2\frac{2}{3}$ **h.** $3\frac{1}{5} > \frac{12}{5}$

Brain-teaser Ali
Brain-buster $\frac{3}{4}$ a pizza

Page 43

Check

1   **a.** $\frac{3}{5}$ **b.** $\frac{5}{7}$ **c.** $\frac{4}{4}$ or 1   **d.** $1\frac{1}{5}$

2   **a.** $\frac{1}{6}$ **b.** $\frac{3}{8}$ **c.** $\frac{2}{4} = \frac{1}{2}$ **d.** $\frac{6}{20} = \frac{3}{10}$

3   **a.** $\frac{3}{4}$ **b.** $\frac{5}{6}$ **c.** $\frac{3}{6} = \frac{1}{2}$ **d.** $\frac{29}{30}$

4   **a.** $\frac{1}{4}$ **b.** $\frac{1}{6}$ **c.** $\frac{1}{6}$ **d.** $\frac{19}{30}$

Brain-teaser $\frac{3}{6}$ or $\frac{1}{2}$ a pizza

Brain-buster $\frac{5}{12}$

Page 45

Check

1   **a.** 5   **b.** 2   **c.** 6   **d.** 10

2   **a.** $2\frac{1}{2}$ or $2\frac{2}{4}$ **b.** $1\frac{1}{2}$ **c.** $1\frac{5}{7}$ **d.** $3\frac{1}{3}$

3   **a.** 7   **b.** $4\frac{1}{2}$ **c.** $10\frac{5}{6}$ **d.** $26\frac{2}{3}$

Brain-teaser $19\frac{1}{2}$ logs
Brain-buster 8 laps

Page 47

Check

1   **a.**

Fraction	$\frac{1}{10}$	$\frac{2}{10}$	$\frac{3}{10}$	$\frac{4}{10}$	$\frac{5}{10}$	$\frac{6}{10}$	$\frac{7}{10}$	$\frac{8}{10}$	$\frac{9}{10}$	$\frac{10}{10}$
Decimal	0.1	0.2	0.3	0.4	0.5	0.6	0.7	0.8	0.9	1.0

     b.

Fraction	$\frac{1}{5}$	$\frac{2}{5}$	$\frac{3}{5}$	$\frac{4}{5}$	$\frac{5}{5}$
Decimal	0.2	0.4	0.6	0.8	1

2   **a.** 0.5   **b.** 0.75   **c.** 0.1

3   **a.** $\frac{1}{4}$ **b.** $\frac{7}{10}$ **c.** $\frac{4}{10}$

Brain-teaser $\frac{3}{4}$
Brain-buster No, one quarter = 0.25

Page 49

Check

1

Fraction name	Decimal Fraction	Decimal	Decimal name
five tenths	$\frac{5}{10}$	0.5	zero point five
twenty-three hundredths	$\frac{23}{100}$	0.23	zero point two three
four hundred and thirty-five thousandths	$\frac{435}{1000}$	0.435	zero point four three five
Three tenths	$\frac{3}{10}$	0.3	zero point three
Eighty-six hundredths	$\frac{86}{100}$	0.86	zero point eight six
Five hundred and seven thousandths	$\frac{507}{1000}$	0.507	zero point five zero seven
Eight tenths	$\frac{8}{10}$	0.8	zero point eight
One hundred and thirty-two thousandths	$\frac{132}{1000}$	0.132	zero point one three two
Thirty-nine hundredths	$\frac{39}{100}$	0.39	zero point three nine
One hundred and four thousandths	$\frac{104}{1000}$	0.104	zero point one zero four

Brain-teaser $\frac{87}{100}$, 0.204

Brain-buster $\frac{765}{1000}$, 0.765

Page 51

Check

1   **a.** 0.465   **b.** 0.204

2   **a.** 0.6   **b.** 0.12   **c.** 0.325

3   **a.** zero point three nine five   **b.** zero point six zero two
    c. zero point zero zero five

4   **a.** 0.002, 0.084, 0.146, 0.327, 0.5, 0.75, 0.807, 0.999
    b. Check numbers on number line are accurately positioned.

Brain-teaser Bugs B and C
Brain-buster Bug C: 0.009cm, Bug B: 0.029cm, Bug D: 0.031cm, Bug A: 0.101cm

Page 53

Check

1   **a.** 1   **b.** 2   **c.** 5   **d.** 0   **e.** 1   **f.** 7   **g.** 12   **h.** 7

2   **a.** 0.8   **b.** 0.8   **c.** 0.5   **d.** 0.8   **e.** 5.6   **f.** 4.1
    g. 12.8   **h.** 7.0

3   Rounding decimals makes it easier to calculate amounts, but the answers will not be accurate.

Brain-teaser

Day	Monday	Tuesday	Wednes-day	Thursday	Friday	Saturday
Money	£52.14	£45.61	£60.13	£46.50	£72.24	£35.51
Rounded	£52	£46	£60	£47	£72	£36

Brain-buster More, because he rounds up more than he rounds down (rounded to £313; exact amount £312.13).

Page 55

Check

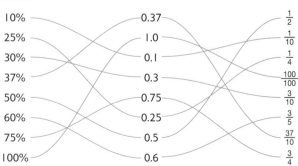

Brain-teaser 15 have dinners, 10% have sandwiches
Brain-buster 12 children go home for lunch. This is 40% of the class.

MEASUREMENT

Page 57

Check

1   **a.**

cm	m
100	1
35	0.35
450	4.5
1000	10
8000	80
900	9
90	0.9
27	0.27

b.

mm	cm
10	1
25	2.5
52	5.2
100	10
300	30
170	17
60	6
2	0.2

c.

m	km
1000	1
250	0.25
5350	5.35
10,000	10
6000	6
4500	4.5
1350	1.35
4	0.004

2

Imperial	Metric
1 inch	2.54cm
5 inches	12.7cm

Imperial	Metric
10 inches	25.4cm
1 mile	1.61km

Imperial	metric
100 miles	161km
300 miles	483km

Brain-teaser 4.8m
Brain-buster 5.35km

Page 59

Check

1   **a.** 10cm   **b.** 8cm   **c.** 12cm

2   **a.** 24cm   **b.** 24cm

3

shape	formula	length	width	perimeter
rectangle	p = 2(l+ w)	6mm	3mm	18mm
square	p = 4s	2.5mm	2.5mm	10m (1cm)

4   **a.** w = 1cm   **b.** w = 8m

Brain-teaser 3m
Brain-buster 7m

Page 61

Check

1   **a.** approx 15cm^2 **b.** approx 8cm^2 **c.** approx 13cm^2

2   **a.** 108cm^2 **b.** 49m^2 **c.** 300m^2

3   **a.** a rectangle, length 5cm and width 1cm   **b.** a square of side 5cm   **c.** a square of side 6m   **d.** a rectangle, length 17km and width 9km

Brain-teaser 14m^2
Brain-buster 81,000 potatoes

Page 63

Check

1

object	grams	kilograms
child	50,000g	50kg
dog	12,000g	12kg
pencil	75g	0.075kg
book	408g	0.408kg

2

object	milliltres	litres
teapot	1250ml	1.25l
sink	8500ml	8.5l
mug	125ml	0.125l
thimble	12ml	0.012l

3   **a.** 483g or 0.483kg   **b.** 137ml or 0.137l
    c. 50.408kg or 50,408g   **d.** 1.262l or 1262ml

Brain-teaser 20kg
Brain-buster 851ml or 0.851l

Check

12-hour	midnight	2:10am	9:15am	noon	3:30pm	9pm	11:59pm
24-hour	00:00	02:10	09:15	12:00	15:30	21:00	23:59

2 **a.** 180 minutes **b.** 48 hours **c.** 84 days
   d. 1460 days (or +1 if leap year included)
   e. 1 hour 40 minutes **f.** 4 days 4 hours
   g. 3 hours 45 minutes **h.** 1 year 135 days

3 **a.** 11 hours and 55 minutes **b.** 4 days 12 hours and 41
   minutes **c.** 9 days 2 hours and 58 minutes

Brain-teaser 8:37am
Brain-buster 604,800 seconds

Page 67

Check

1

Pence	200p	135p	6325p	9p	10,903p
Pounds	£2	£1.35	£63.25	£0.09	£109.03

2

Pounds	£4	£2.56	£0.12	£82	£403.20
Pence	400p	256p	12p	8200p	40,320p

3 **a.** £7.77 **b.** £22.15 **c.** £1.70 **d.** £41.73 **e.** £6.70 **f.**
   £70.40 **g.** £12.50 **h.** £7.70

Brain-teaser £15.75
Brain-buster £600

GEOMETRY

Page 69

Check

1 **a.** 90° right-angle **b.** 130° obtuse angle **c.** 65° acute angle

2 **a.**   **b.**   **c.**

   right-angle   reflex angle   acute angle

Brain-teaser Aaron can place his ruler alongside the line to
decide if it is more or less than 180°. Over 180° is reflex, less
than 180° is acute or obtuse. If he rests his pencil at right angles
to his ruler this will give him a right angle. Angles less than this
will be acute; more than this but less than 180° will be obtuse.
Brain-buster Because the angles on a straight line add up to
180°.

Page 71

Check

1 **a.**   **b.**   **c.**

   d.   **e.**

Brain-teaser 3, 270°
Brain-buster 180° anticlockwise

Page 73

Check

1 **a.** regular triangle **b.** regular hexagon **c.** irregular
   quadrilateral **d.** irregular pentagon

2 Because the sides are not all the same length.

3 **a.** square **b.** parallelogram **c.** kite **d.** rectangle
   e. trapezium **f.** rhombus

Brain-teaser Both long sides should be labelled 6cm, both short
sides should be labelled 4cm. All four angles should be labelled
90°.

Page 75

Check

1

triangular prism	cylinder	cube	cuboid
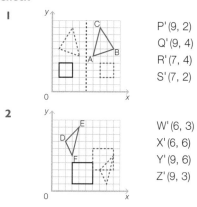			

2 **a.** sphere **b.** cube **c.** cone **d.** cylinder
   e. triangular prism **f.** cuboid

Brain-teaser cuboid
Brain-buster The cylinder would hold more water than the
cone because it is the same width all the way along, but the cone
gets narrower.

Page 77

Check

1

   P' (9, 2)
   Q' (9, 4)
   R' (7, 4)
   S' (7, 2)

2

   W' (6, 3)
   X' (6, 6)
   Y' (9, 6)
   Z' (9, 3)

Brain-buster If the mirror line is horizontal the point moves up
or down, so the y-coordinate changes. If it is vertical they move
left or right, so the x-coordinate changes. Find the distance the
point is from the mirror line, then move the x or y coordinate by
double the amount.

STATISTICS

Page 79

Check

1 **a.**

   b. 3 weeks **c.** 8 weeks **d.** 6 weeks

Brain-teaser Highest temperature: 18°C
When was the temperature highest? 8am
Brain-buster Find the difference between the highest and lowest
temperatures: 16°C

Page 81

1 **a.** Earth **b.** Mars **c.** Mercury **d.** Earth and Mars

2 **a.** number 7 bus **b.** every half hour **c.** 3 minutes
   d. The train station could be further away than the
   supermarket, or the number 6 bus may have to wait at the
   train station for a set amount of time.

Brain-teaser The number 7 at 10:15
Brain-buster 14:45

Glossary

12-hour clock Time that uses 12 hours, with am before 12 noon, and pm after.

24-hour clock Time that uses 24 hours for the time; does not need am or pm, 5.30pm is written as 17:30.

2D Two-dimensional, a term used for shapes with no depth, usually drawn on paper or viewed on a screen.

3D Three-dimensional, a term used for solid shapes with length, depth and height.

A

Acute angle An angle measuring between 0° and 90°.

Adjacent Near or next to something, usually used for talking about angles, sides or faces.

Analogue clock Shows the time with hands on a dial.

Angle The measure of the gap between lines that meet, or the amount by which something turns; measured in degrees.

Anticlockwise Rotating in the opposite direction to the hands of a clock.

Approximate A number found by rounding or estimating

Area The amount of surface covered by a shape.

Axis (plural axes) The horizontal and vertical lines on a graph.

B

Base 10 The structure of our number system; also called powers of 10 because all numbers are based on the powers of 10: 10, 100, 1000, and so on.

C

Clockwise Rotating in the same direction as the hands of a clock.

Coordinates Numbers that give the position of a point on a graph, (x, y).

Cube number A number multiplied by itself twice, such as $2 \times 2 \times 2 = 2^3 = 8$.

D

Decimal fraction A decimal number, whose fraction equivalent has a denominator of a power of 10. For example, 0.5, 0.34, 0.429.

Decimal places Decimals can be written to one or more decimal places: 3.214 has three decimal places.

Decimal point The dot used to separate the fractional part of a number from the whole.

Denominator The number on the bottom of a fraction.

Difference The amount between two numbers.

Digits Our number system uses ten digits, 0–9, to represent all our numbers.

Digital clock A clock that shows time using digits rather than using hands on a dial; can show 12-hour or 24-hour time.

E

Edge The line where two faces of a 3D shape meet.

Equivalent fractions Fractions with different numerators and denominators that represent the same amount, such as $\frac{1}{2}$ and $\frac{2}{4}$.

Estimate To use information to get an approximate answer.

Even numbers Numbers that can be divided by 2; they end in 0, 2, 4, 6 or 8.

Exchange Alternative terminology for carry/borrow used in formal written methods for addition, subtraction, multiplication and division.

F

Face The flat or curved areas of 3D shapes.

Factor A number that will divide exactly into a particular number. For example, 1, 2, 3, 4, 6 and 12 are the factors of 12.

I

Imperial units Units for measuring length, capacity and mass before decimal units were created; length uses inches, feet and miles, capacity uses fluid ounces and pints, and mass uses pounds and tons.

Improper fraction (Also called a vulgar fraction) is a fraction with a numerator larger than its denominator.

Irregular polygon A 2D shape which does not have identical sides and angles.

Isometric drawing A technique for drawing 3D shapes on flat surfaces.

L

Line graphs A graph that shows how something changes over time, like height, temperature or speed.

M

Mental methods Methods for accurately solving calculations without writing them down.

Million The number 1,000,000; one thousand thousand.

Mixed number A whole number and a fraction, such as $3\frac{2}{5}$.

Multiple A number made by multiplying two numbers together, such as. 6 is a multiple of both 2 and 3.

N

Negative number A number less than zero.

Numerator The top number of a fraction; the numerator is divided by the denominator.

O

Obtuse angle An angle measuring more than 90° and less than180°.

Odd numbers Numbers that cannot be divided by 2; they end in 1, 3, 5, 7 or 9.

P

Percentage A number expressed as a fraction out of 100, and represented using the % symbol, meaning percent. For example, 58%.

Perimeter The distance around the outside edge of a closed shape.

Polygon Any straight-sided 2D shape.

Positive number A number greater than zero.

Powers of 10 The structure of our number system; sometimes called Base ten. Powers of 10 are numbers that are made by multiplying 10 by 10 a number of times. For example, 100 is 10 × 10 or 10 to the power of 2 (10^2), 1000 is 10 × 10 × 10 or 10 to the power of 3 (10^3).

Prime factor A factor that is also a prime number; 3 is a prime factor of 12.

Prime number A whole number that can only be divided by itself and by 1 with no remainder (1 itself is not a prime number).

Proportion The fraction of an amount, such as *eight out of nine people wore red*.

R

Reflection A mirror image of a point or shape, in a mirror line, on a graph.

Reflex angle An angle measuring between 180° and 360°.

Regular polygon A 2D shape with all sides and angles identical.

Roman numerals The system of letters used by the Romans to represent numbers, still sometimes used on clock faces and to represent years.

Rounding Whole numbers are often rounded to the nearest power of ten, and decimals to the nearest whole number, tenth or hundredth to make calculations easier.

S

Square number A number multiplied by itself, such as. 3 × 3 = 9 or $3^2 = 9$.

Symbol A sign used for an operation or relationship in mathematics, such as +, −, ×, ÷, =, < and >.

Symmetrical A symmetrical shape is one that is identical either side of a mirror line.

T

Translation Movement of points or shapes on a graph by moving each point by the same amount and in the same direction.

V

Vertex (plural *vertices*) The corner of a 3D shape where edges meet.

Multiplication table

x	1	2	3	4	5	6	7	8	9	10	11	12
1	1	2	3	4	5	6	7	8	9	10	11	12
2	2	4	6	8	10	12	14	16	18	20	22	24
3	3	6	9	12	15	18	21	24	27	30	33	36
4	4	8	12	16	20	24	28	32	36	40	44	48
5	5	10	15	20	25	30	35	40	45	50	55	60
6	6	12	18	24	30	36	42	48	54	60	66	72
7	7	14	21	28	35	42	49	56	63	70	77	84
8	8	16	24	32	40	48	56	64	72	80	88	96
9	9	18	27	36	45	54	63	72	81	90	99	108
10	10	20	30	40	50	60	70	80	90	100	110	120
11	11	22	33	44	55	66	77	88	99	110	121	132
12	12	24	36	48	60	72	84	96	108	120	132	144